Heaven's Cowboy

By

Theresa Freeman Carpenter

ISBN: 1461139317
ISBN-13: 9781461139317

Visit www.createspace.com/3596657 to order
additional copies.

To Corbin

I love you and miss you very much. I'm still your biggest fan.

Corbin Carpenter
March 9, 1991 – September 22, 2010

Picture taken March 2010

(courtesy of Kathy Howerton/Just the Way You Are)

Preface

"Faith makes things possible…not easy."

My husband, Dewitt, and I have often talked about faith and how important it is in our daily walk with God. We both agree that we do not understand how people go through even the ordinary trials each of us face daily, much less the tragedies in our lives without Jesus' arms wrapped tightly around us. Without God's love and mercy to see us through, not only in times of extreme need such as sickness, death, etc., I would find it impossible to function.

I believe that God sometimes provides specific means for our faith to grow. He did this in a big way in our lives on July 25, 2008. Without a doubt, our faith has grown stronger and has allowed us to survive several life changing tragedies since that time. No, it has not been easy to deal with these tragedies, but our faith has been strengthened and we know God has never left us. We continue to lean on Him daily to survive one day at a time.

Each of us face hard times and it is up to us as individuals to use these trials and tribulations as a tool to make us stronger in our faith and in our daily walk with the Lord. It is our responsibility to share our experiences with others in hopes it will help someone else through a difficult time in their lives.

I would like to share with you our story of tragedy, triumph, trials and the faith that is bringing us through.

Chapter 1

It was July 25, 2008. The day started as any other at a rodeo. As if it were needed, I was giving last minute advice to our seventeen-year-old son, Corbin, on how he should cover the bull he was about to ride that morning. It was the usual advice, ride jump for jump, chest out, etc. Corbin gave me one of his "I don't know what makes you an authority on bull ridin'" looks. It was followed by my teasing saying something like, "Well, at least that's the way I used to do it when I rode bulls," knowing full well I had never ridden a bull in my life other than playing around at the barn when we were kids jumping on the backs of some calves or steers.

Today, however, was not just 'any other day at the rodeo.' It was the second go around at the 2008 National High School Finals Rodeo (NHSFR) in Farmington, New Mexico. Corbin was riding his second bull in hopes of securing a spot in the Championship round (or short go, as it is sometimes called) and winning the 2008 Champion Bull Rider title. Just two days before, Corbin had covered (a bull riding term meaning successfully ridden) his first bull receiving a score. He knew without a doubt that one more successful ride would place him in the championship round. He was hungry for this win more than ever. Just one short year before, Corbin finished the year in ninth place at the 2007 NHSFR in Springfield, Illinois. At that time, he was awarded a generous scholarship from PBR (Professional Bull Riders) and a "Top Ten Bull Rider" trophy belt buckle. Shortly after the win, a lady asked him if he was going to wear his new buckle. He replied, "No ma'am, I'll be back next year to get the Champion buckle and I'll wear that one."

Most of us would think a ninth place finish in the world would be an awesome accomplishment, especially for a high school sophomore, but not Corbin. He said even a second place finish is considered the first place loser. Good point, I guess. Nonetheless, his dad and I were elated at his achievement.

∽

My husband (Corbin's dad), Dewitt, had already called that morning. He gave his last words of encouragement to Corbin before the big ride. Back home, Dewitt and I have a dirt contracting business and a new project had started the week prior to our leaving home for the national finals. As badly as he wanted to be with us that week, it was a big job, and with Louisiana weather being as unpredictable as it is, he felt he needed to get the work started while the weather was favorable. Corbin, Colt (our youngest son, then ten years old) and I had already been gone from home for over a week. The week prior to the NHSFR, Corbin was competing at the International Finals Youth Rodeo (IFYR) in Shawnee, Oklahoma, where he was a member of the Bloomer Trailer High School Rodeo Team.

While in Shawnee, Corbin had bucked off his first bull but had a great ride on his second bull, scoring a seventy-one, and missing the championship round by only a half point. It was heartbreaking for each of us. Not only was Corbin in the business to win but he wanted to do his very best as a Bloomer Trailer Rodeo Team member. Although not making it to the short round, he didn't allow himself to become discouraged and kept his focus on his upcoming job the following week in Farmington.

ை

The first part of the week in Farmington had not been a successful one for Shane Hood, a fellow Louisiana bull rider and one of Corbin's closest friends. When we arrived at the NHSFR during the wee hours of the morning on Sunday, July 21, 2008, Shane wasn't feeling well. The next morning found him at the first aid station set up on sight at the rodeo, where he was diagnosed with possible food poisoning. After giving Shane medication, he felt better for a while, but by night his condition was once again diminishing. The first round of the rodeo would begin the next day. Shane, unfortunately, was scheduled to ride his first bull then. However, the rodeo committee allowed him to postpone his ride until Wednesday since he had proof of having been treated at the hospital. Because he was so weak from being ill, he failed to get anything accomplished on either of his bulls. What a disappointment to each of us, especially Shane. The Hood's planned to start for home on Thursday morning, July 25th following Corbin's ride.

Corbin knew he had to complete the ride that Thursday morning in order to qualify for the short round. Our plans were to follow the Hood family back to Louisiana if Corbin bucked off. However, if he covered his bull that morning, he would ride two days later in Saturday's short round. Obviously the latter was our goal.

Corbin gathered his gear bag as we walked out of the hotel room carrying the rest of our luggage. The boys and I arrived at the arena and I dropped Corbin off near the gate so he wouldn't have to carry his heavy rigging bag as far. Colt and I would have to park quite a distance from the entrance. I told Corbin I loved him and I watched him walk away with his green rigging bag secured on his back. As he walked away, I read the words "2006 LHSRA Rookie of the Year Bull Rider" that was stitched onto his gear bag. Little did I know, this may be the last time I would see him walk away from me.

⁓

I knew Corbin wasn't feeling his best. He woke up that morning with his stomach not feeling well. We later pieced the puzzle together to realize Shane, Corbin and a couple of other guys had eaten at the same fast food restaurant in Shawnee the day before we left. We assumed that was the culprit of Shane's food poisoning and now perhaps Corbin's stomach problems. Also, the week previous while competing at the IFYR, Corbin took a shot from his first bull leaving a big knot on the back of his head. I wasn't in Shawnee when he rode his first bull, so he didn't bother to tell me about getting hit but rather told his sister. After Corbin and Courtney talked, she called to tell me about his run-in with the bull. Of course, when I talked to him, he down played the whole situation. That is, until I received a call from Kim Bloomer (Bloomer Trailer Manufacturing) who also shared the news. I had not yet made it to Shawnee but talked to Corbin regularly on the phone. When I asked Corbin about the hit, he again played it down like there wasn't much to it, and to a hard headed bull rider, it probably wasn't. Another injury Corbin had sustained even before he left home for Shawnee was to his leg. Corbin left a week before the Shawnee trip to go with professional bull riders and friends, Chris Shivers and Mike White. This was Corbin's third time to help them put on a bull riding school in Sulphur, Louisiana. While there, Corbin got on a few practice bulls in the afternoons after the school was over. I never did know exactly how it happened, and I'm sure it was never intended that I did, but somehow, in the midst of the ride or the dismount thereafter, Corbin hurt his leg. Several months passed before he told me that he thought he had broken the small bone in the lower part of his leg. He wouldn't tell us because he thought we may not let him compete at the IFYR and the national finals. Either way, Corbin wasn't going into this round at his best that morning but, regardless, determined to do whatever it took to cover every bull.

The New Mexico sun was bright that morning and shining hard on the on-looking crowd. I thought they would never call Corbin's name to ride, and the anticipation was killing me. I had talked to Dewitt a few times already. He was anxious to hear from me with the results of Corbin's ride. He said he had a strong feeling that Corbin was going to cover his second bull, and was already wondering how in the world he would get to New Mexico for Saturday's short round. I was taking careful consideration that my video camera was set just right so I could get all of the action. Corbin always wanted to watch his ride afterwards to see how he could improve the next time. I knew he and Dewitt would want to soak up every second of the action.

Finally, nearing lunch time, Corbin's name was called and the gate opened.

The day prior to his "wreck" with M33, Corbin went trout fishing with Shane Hood and his dad, Randy Hood, near Farmington, NM

Chapter 2

When Dewitt and I were dating and after we were married in 1981, he continued to team rope and both of us competed at an occasional local play day or rodeo in open events. I even showed a couple of our horses at halter. Our time on horseback was mostly out of necessity, checking and working our cattle. Likewise, our children, Lee, Courtney, Corbin and Colt were raised riding horses and working cattle. When Lee and Courtney were young, they rode quite a bit, but by the time Courtney was nine-years-old, she became very involved with the Junior Beefmaster Breeders Association (JBBA). At that time, Dewitt and I turned our focus more toward improving our purebred Beefmaster herd and hauling Courtney and her string of show cattle across the south to compete. She was very successful with her exhibition of cattle and in showmanship. At the annual JBBA National Finals, Courtney was named Reserve Champion national public speaker five years running. Through the years, she was also awarded numerous other national awards such as Champion Junior Showman and Reserve Champion

Marketing Team, an award she shared with long time friend, Beth House. She was a member of the Champion Cattle Judging Team and received other prestigious honors through the years. We have several walls in our home adorned with plaques, trophies and banners to prove her dedication and consistency. By the time Courtney was in high school, she was elected to serve on the National Junior Beefmaster Breeders Board of Directors. Lee was never very interested in showing cattle and was simply satisfied riding his favorite horse, Prince, at home.

ᦀ

Even as a young child, Corbin was comical, and I can't remember when he didn't have those 'one liners' and made sarcastic comments that would make you crack up! Several stories come to mind when Corbin was about four-years-old. Prior to his cattle showing career, we were in Raymond, Mississippi at a Beefmaster cattle show. It was typical Louisiana June weather, very hot. Corbin and Ethan House were playing in the dirt and rocks while the show was in progress. They were playing outside of a barn just down the hillside from the show arena, and we could easily watch them as we were "taking care of business" at the show arena. Living in such a rural area, we were slow getting the 9-1-1 emergency service, but it had finally arrived in our area and we were teaching our children to dial it in the event of an emergency. During the cattle show this particular day, Ethan, who was the same age as Corbin, came running to me saying "Mrs. Theresa, Corbin said call 9-1-1 FAST!" I could see my son sitting in the dirt and knew it wasn't a terrible emergency but nonetheless took off toward him. When I got close enough to him, I asked what was the emergency?

Corbin said, "Call 9-1-1, call 9-1-1: I have hurt my toe and I've got to have some help here!!"

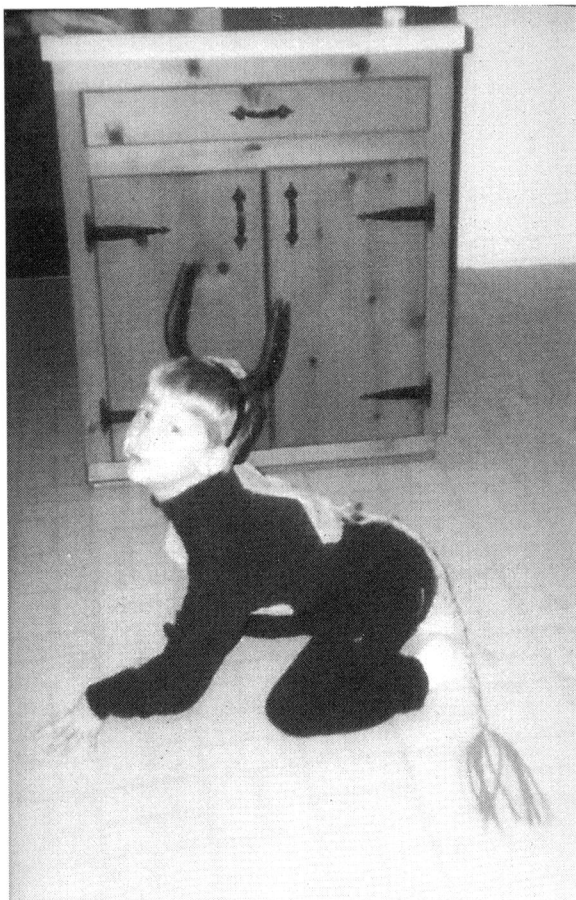

At three-years-old, Corbin was a bull for Halloween. He had bulls and bull riding in his blood early!

Heaven's Cowboy

In Corbin's words, "I know this sounds a little random, but…." this story, I believe is one of those worthy of inclusion in this book because it depicts his comedic personality, even at a young age. Corbin was at the age where he could be left alone for short periods of time while he was taking his nightly bath. Especially considering our hall bathroom is the first room down the hallway from my kitchen, and when the door is open, I can hear all that goes on there. This particular night, I could hear the water splashing as if a tornado were in that bathroom! I stepped around the corner to see what my little "tornado" was doing and found he was playing with his trucks and obviously had them in four wheel drive as they did tricks in the water. After a couple of minutes of taking all of this in, Corbin realized I was watching him. Immediately, he gave me the 'deer in the headlights' look which had "I'm busted" written all over his face. The bathroom was soaked with water from the ceiling down. In a stern voice, I said, "Corbin Carpenter!"

He started shaking his head and in as calm and slow of a voice as he could muster, said, "Awe… now… don't go a gettin' all mad."

What do you say to that? I laughed and cleaned up the mess.

Of course, one story leads to another, plus this story is important to Colt. Although Colt had not been born when it originated, he is very aware of it as it has been an ongoing joke at our house for many years and still is today. It was along the time Corbin was three or four-years-old. I heard him talking as he was playing alone in the dirt in our backyard. Listening carefully, I could tell he had an imaginary friend. I asked who he was talking to and he simply replied, "Tommy."

I nonchalantly questioned him further and he explained how he and Tommy were moving dirt with their trucks and building a pond. "Tommy" ate with us, took baths with Corbin, and played with him almost daily. This "friend" stayed around our house for years until he eventually went away.

Corbin was about twelve or thirteen-years-old and it had been several years since "Tommy" had visited. I can't remember what the particular circumstances were but it was one of those times when something had been done and no one owned up to it, for example, tracking mud into the house. Knowing either Corbin or Colt had done whatever it was, as we mothers sometime do, especially when caught off guard, I screamed, "Who did this?"

Without missing a beat, Corbin said with a most serious look on his face, "Tommy did it!"

"Who is Tommy?" I screamed back.

"You remember, Tommy, my imaginary friend" replied Corbin.

All three of us fell out with laughter and from that time on, Tommy seems to do a lot around my house and gets in more trouble imaginable!

∽

At four-years-old, Corbin had become an active member of the JBBA at which time he showed his first heifer and competed in the annual national finals public speaking contest.   I will never forget his public speaking debut when he was a mere four-years-old. I dressed him in a brand new pair of starched jeans, a crisp white dress shirt with a red tie and navy sports coat. Of course his cowboy 'dress up' wardrobe wouldn't have been complete without his hat. and favorite cowboy boots. He was very nervous to speak in front of a large crowd despite our many hours of practice so Dewitt asked if he wanted to take his 'notes' on stage with him. Corbin agreed. While he was on stage behind the microphone reciting his speech word for word, he kept his eyes on the paper he was holding. He never missed a beat and spoke with perfection. We were sorely disappointed at the awards banquet when his name was not called to be in the top ten in the five years and under age group. One of the judges came to me after the banquet and said he wanted to place Corbin in the top ten but couldn't because he 'read' his speech. You can imagine his shock and regret when I told him Corbin was simply holding the paper, he couldn't read a single word!

Corbin showed cattle a few more years but quickly found it was not fast paced enough to suit him. By the time Courtney graduated high school and moved on to college, Corbin was done with cattle exhibition.

Corbin showing off his new chaps while at a cattle show in Tyler, Texas. It was obvious, even at four years old, he would rather ride them than show them!

At about eight or so years old, Corbin decided he wanted a really "cool" nickname like The Lone Ranger had. As we were driving along one day, he matter-of-factly declared that from now on, he wanted to be called "Lightnin' Bolt" because it sounded really tough. He instructed me that anytime I was addressing him, to say Lightening Bolt rather than Corbin. I played along. Corbin and I were in my truck going somewhere a day or two later and as we approached an intersection, I began looking to the right for any on-coming traffic. I asked, "What's coming on your side, Corbin?"

Corbin said, "You'll have to ask what's coming, Lightnin' Bolt, because Corbin is not in here today."

Even today, we still say as we approach intersections, "Nothin's comin' Lightening Bolt's way."

∽

When Corbin was nine-years-old and Colt was three, a group of adults, Dewitt and I included, decided to form a local junior rodeo. It was then that the Lazy T Youth Rodeo Association (LTYRA) was born. Both Corbin and Colt wanted to compete in every event in their age groups. The rodeo was structured so that each time a contestant placed in an event, he or she won a little paycheck and earned points. The contestant with the most points earned at the end of the season would be named Champion of the particular event. Or, if they competed in enough qualifying events, had the opportunity to be crowned the all coveted "Champion All Around Cowboy or Cowgirl" and would take home a trophy saddle to prove their success.

Although both of our younger boys had been on a horse all their lives, they had never ridden rough stock. Colt was only three-years-old when he started riding sheep at the first Lazy T rodeo. Corbin was nine and his first rough stock experience was atop a steer. Because of his age, he had to compete on steers for a couple of years but his heart was focused on the junior bulls he would soon grow into. Corbin didn't like riding steers at all. Because of their size and structure, steers tend to have a very bony back and with Corbin's tall, lanky frame and lack of padding on his bottom side, it made for an uncomfortable eight seconds. He was elated when he could start competing on bulls and leave the steer riding to the younger fellows.

At the end of the first LTYRA season, Colt, who was four by then, won his first saddle by capturing the title of the five-year-old and under Champion All Around Cowboy. Although Corbin had a great season, he missed the title by only a few points but won the Reserve Champion All Around Cowboy. Both boys won champion and reserve champion in individual events such as rough stock, barrels, poles and roping. Over the next few years throughout the life of the LTYRA, both boys brought home numerous awards, a pile of money, and a list of titles, including each of them winning several "Champion All Around Cowboy" titles and the saddles that went with them.

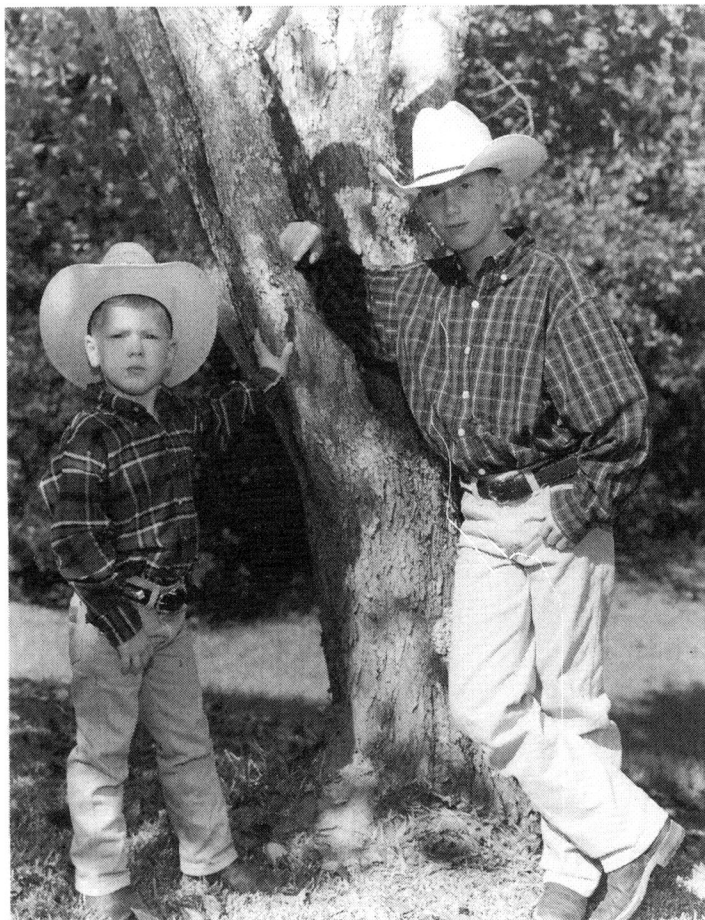

Colt and Corbin Carpenter, ages 3 and 10 years old, respectively

It wasn't long before both Corbin and Colt were competing in several youth circuit rodeos in the area in addition to the Lazy T. I will never forget a conversation Corbin and I had one day as he told me that he had ridden bulls long enough that he was actually able to THINK about what he was doing. He said up until that point, he had merely been trying to hold on, maybe only concentrating on one or two things, for example, staying on his rope or keeping his toes out, etc. He said he was finally coming into a form of riding where he could think about what the bull was doing so he could counteract the movement. I knew then, bull riding would very much be a part of his future.

Colt, age 7, and Corbin, age 14
Fall 2005

The boys were also riding in a little local series put on by the Catahoula Riding Club. It was held bi-monthly in the Jonesville arena. When the arena was built in the early 1980's, it was the largest outdoor facility in the south. As board members, we host an annual professional rodeo, The Black River Roundup. However, for the remainder of the year the arena is utilized by the youth rodeos. Qualified bull fighters were practically non-existent at these little junior playdays so whoever wanted to try their hand when the steers and small junior bulls bucked out were more than welcomed. Tyler Myers, a friend of my boys who was about two years younger than Corbin loved the rough stock arena and could ride the hair off of a steer. His rough stock career was short lived as his mom wasn't very fond of his choice of events and strongly encouraged him to focus on roping. This particular day, Tyler was trying his hand at bull fighting. Corbin came out on this little junior bull and Tyler was in front with his hand out in the bull's face, trying to get him to turn. As Corbin was riding, he realized Tyler was 'in the line of fire' so to speak and remembered thinking "You better move, you better move...up, you didn't move," as the little bull ran directly over Tyler.

Once we realized Tyler was not hurt and Corbin told us the story, we laughed uncontrollably and have never let Tyler forget it! Of course, the picture that was taken helps to keep the story alive!

Tyler Myers trying his hand at bullfighting. Corbin riding a junior bull at the Catahoula Riding Club Junior Rodeo. Tyler's grandmother shot this photo just before Tyler lost his footing and went down! Spring 2006.

Heaven's Cowboy

The year 2006, when Corbin was a sophomore, was the first year he attempted to ride a bull during the Black River Roundup Rodeo which was sanctioned by the Louisiana Rodeo Cowboys Association (LRCA). However, it wasn't until the following year that he covered his bull and placed second. He had led the rodeo until the very last rider scored a couple of points higher. Only once in the history of the Black River Roundup Rodeo has a Jonesville cowboy won the bull riding. With an awesome ride in 2005, our friend, Lee White, took the title. The year following his second place finish, 2008, Corbin bucked off of a black mottle-faced bull just in front of the chutes. He landed directly in front of the bull. It seemed as though time stood still as Corbin jumped up and he and the bull were standing within inches, staring eye to eye. Thankfully, the bull opted to turn left rather than run over Corbin. Each year, beginning in 2006, in addition to bull riding, Corbin also team roped and/or calf roped during the competition and although stopping the clock several times, he never placed in either of those events.

❦

When Corbin was twelve-years-old, we realized he had a gift with horses and by the time he was fourteen, he had his own business of breaking and training them. Dewitt and I have always owned horses. We started raising them within a few months of our marriage and have always kept quite a few on our place. One in particular was a little bay mare that Corbin barn named "Pud." Pud's American Quarter Horse Association (AQHA) registered name is Lady's Devil Girl. She was as mean as a rattle snake to other horses and in the natural pecking order of the horses, there was no doubt she demanded their respect. We bought this mare when she was a long yearling and even then, she 'ruled the roost' on the place. We had kept her in a pasture along with several other horses that weren't being used often. Almost daily one of us took a sack of feed and poured small piles on the ground just to keep the horses coming up and to inspect them, making sure none had been injured or were sick.

Everyday they would start running toward us when they saw us coming to the barn, knowing they were about to get their daily treat. This particular day, for whatever reason, Pud was extremely overpowering, wheeling around to the other horses and kicking. Once, she whirled around kicking another mare, and I found it was too close for comfort for me. When Dewitt came home that night, I told him we were getting rid of that 'mean little wench.' I knew she meant no intentional harm to us but accidents do happen. For whatever reason, we didn't sell her and Corbin soon began working with her. Corbin and Pud quickly bonded, and there was no denying that soon he could do more with that mare than anyone else at any given time. This never changed.

Theresa Freeman Carpenter

Corbin and Pud in an April 2009 photo

(photo courtesy of Cindy Thompson Photography)

When Corbin entered the eighth grade, the Louisiana High School Rodeo Association (LHSRA) had put into place the Wrangler Division which was for junior high school students, sixth through eighth grades. At that time, it was sponsored by the Wrangler Jean Company. Corbin was excited to compete on this level and I'm sure we were among the first to submit an application that year. After traveling to the six or seven Wrangler Division rodeos and the state finals, Corbin ended the year sitting fifth place in bull riding, not the finish he had hoped for. However, by this time, Pud had become an accomplished calf roping horse and he and Corbin roped their way to compete at the Inaugural Wrangler Division National Finals Rodeo in Gallup, New Mexico. Corbin had finished the year sitting third in the state and the top four were eligible to compete at the national finals. Corbin's name went down in the record books as being the very first calf roper at the very first junior high national finals . . . talk about putting pressure on a guy! As luck would have it, sadly, he missed both calves and although Corbin didn't have a successful national finals, the experience was awesome and one we would never forget.

The following year (2005-06) Corbin was a rookie in the state high school ranks. He was competing in bull riding, calf roping and team roping with partner, Chrystal Ainsworth from Georgetown, Louisiana.

He competed with much success during the year but didn't gather enough points to make it to the national finals in any of his events. He was, however, named 2006 LHSRA Rookie of the Year Bull Rider.

The school year of 2006-07 Corbin was a sophomore. He and Shane Hood had been riding bulls throughout the year, not only in high school competition but also in numerous jackpot and open events. Many of these events found them competing with pro and semi-pro bull riders. Both Corbin and Shane were riding well that year and had much success winning generous amounts of money and many titles. There wasn't a single bull riding anywhere in the state of Louisiana that the boys didn't know about.

Heaven's Cowboy

A shot of Corbin after having successfully ridden a bull at the Louisiana High School Rodeo at Keatchie, LA, Spring 2007

(Photo courtesy of Burnin Sky Photography)

A fourth place ride at the LHSRA rodeo in Keatchie, LA, spring 2007. His dad and Colt are looking on in the far right corner. Dewitt in the tan jacket wearing sunglasses and Colt in the dark, camoflauge jacket and straw hat to Dewitt's left.

(Photo courtesy of Burnin Sky Photography)

One weekend, there was a big bull riding in the small town of Stonewall, located in western Louisiana near the Texas state line. Of course, both boys wanted to compete and like we spent most of our weekends, we went. When we arrived,

Corbin and Shane went to the pens to survey the bulls and to get their names on the draw sheets. There were both Louisiana and Texas cowboys signed up, many of them professionals and members of the CBR (Championship Bull Riding) and former members of the PBR (Professional Bull Riders). The boys soon realized that many of the bulls had been bucked in the professional ranks of the CBR. Even knowing these facts, neither of these little high school sophomores were intimidated in the least. They were both on top of their game, and came there to do their jobs of winning, and taking home the money. . . and ride they did! Both boys made the short go, and Corbin proved to be the only cowboy who rode all three bulls. Shane rode two bulls, also placing, but I can't recall in what position. When Corbin went to collect his winnings, they paid him $ 666.34 in prize money. He handed the lady back a $1 bill. Looking puzzled, the lady asked what the $1 was for. Corbin told her 666 was the devil's number and he didn't' need that last dollar bill!

∽

Each time Corbin mounted a bull and the gate opened, we knew there was a chance he would become injured. However, Corbin's bull riding talent had become apparent to Dewitt and me and we knew it was in his blood. This kid was going somewhere and going fast. He would 'eat and breathe' bull riding. Of course, having two-time world champion bull rider, Chris Shivers, as a family friend didn't help matters at all! Chris and Corbin spent a good bit of time together roping, hog hunting, working cattle and would often buck out some practice bulls. Chris was raising a few bucking bulls and we, too, had some that we hauled to local rodeos.

One bull we raised particularly stood out among the rest. 'Dirty White Socks' or "Socks" the cowboys had come to call him, was a crowd pleaser and the cowboys viewed him in a "black and white" sense. In other words, they either couldn't wait to draw him and get a shot at riding this infamous bull or they didn't want him at all. There were no "grey" areas for a bull rider when Socks was in the draw. Socks, in bull riding terms, was "the real deal," meaning he had the makings of being one that had a shot of bucking in the pro ranks. At one of Chris and Corbin's practices, we bucked out Socks along with some other bulls. Chris got on Socks and after the ride, confirmed that "Socks was the real deal."

After we were done that night, I asked Chris what Corbin could do to be a better bull rider. He simply replied, "I don't see anything."

Unfortunately, before Socks made it very far, he was struck by lightening and killed. Cowboys still today talk about how rank that bull was. Corbin was only one of four cowboys, including Chris, who ever rode the bull for eight seconds. Even at that, Corbin rode him twice.

∽

By the end of Corbin's sophomore year, he was named LHSRA 2007 Reserve Champion

Bull Rider which would turn out to be his best finish as far as state competition. His buddy, Brice Bache from Zachery, Louisiana, won the Champion title that year and Shane was third place. With a reserve champion win, Corbin was bound for the National High School Finals Rodeo to be held in Springfield, Illinois, later that summer.

At the national finals, Corbin was still riding at the 'top of his game.' He had ridden both long-go-round bulls that week and was going into the short round sitting in a great position to possibly take home the national title. Dewitt had gone behind the chutes with Corbin as he has done hundreds of times before to pull his rope. Colt and I were left sitting on the hillside overlooking the arena. The gate opened and eight seconds later the whistle blew. Corbin was still on board of his third and final bull! I knew this ride would have placed Corbin at least in the top four for the year and maybe better, depending upon how he was scored. Our excitement was cut short when the announcer came over the loud speaker saying Corbin had fouled his bull therefore receiving a 'no score.'   Corbin ended the year in ninth place at the 2007 NHSFR.

A foul is called when the rider touches the bull with his free arm during the course of the ride.   Obviously, this is something a cowboy tries to avoid and sometimes doesn't even know it has happened until it is called by the judge at the end of the ride. I remember once when Corbin was riding at a local event and received a score. He knew he had fouled his bull, and once he dismounted, went to the judge and told him. Of course, the score was pulled from the books, but he sure gained the respect of those judges.

Theresa Freeman Carpenter

Lee, Witt and Caroline Carpenter, Summer 2010

Heaven's Cowboy

Wyatt, Maddison, Kaylee and Courtney
Carpenter Kemp February 2010

(photo courtesy of Cindy Thompson
Photography)

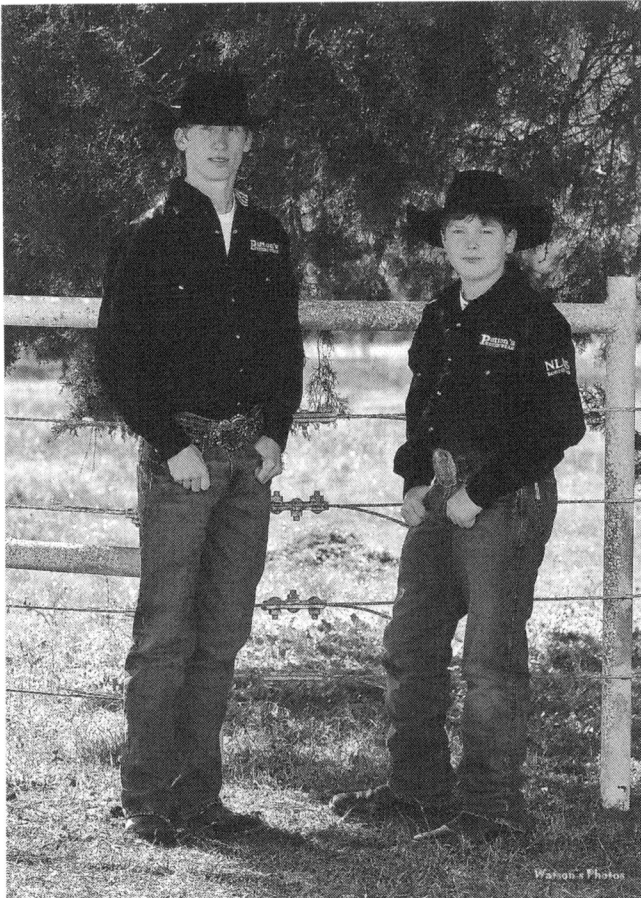

The 2009-10 rodeo season that both Corbin and Colt were on the Northeast Louisiana High School Rodeo team together. Spring 2010

(photo courtesy of Watson's Photography)

Chapter 3

Corbin had seen the big black and white horned bull in the back pens a few days before. He later told me he had watched him in the pen and knew by the way he moved and acted toward the other bulls that he was a bad one and would be real "hooky" for whatever cowboy drew him that week. Little did he know then that he would be the cowboy to draw him for the second-go-round.

Dewitt and I pray for our children daily and I don't know of a single time that I failed to pray for Corbin before and during the time he was riding a bull. Likewise, in all of Corbin's years of riding bulls, I have never known him not to pray prior to a ride. Many times I have seen him lead a group of cowboys in prayer behind the chutes. Corbin came to know the Lord when he was nine-years-old. I was working in Alexandria at the time serving in the capacity of Marketing and Training Officer at Security First National Bank. It was a position I held for eight years before resigning in order to help operate our family businesses. The local college in Alexandria was offering a week long daily summer science camp which included an archeology study. Corbin had always been interested in rocks, fossils, bones and such so I thought this would be a great experience for him. I dropped him off each morning and returned to get him just before lunch. On the way back to my office, I usually ran through the drive-in window at fast food restaurant to pick up lunch for the two of us. On one of these days, I drove up to the window to order, looked over at Corbin who was sitting in the front seat on the passenger side, hunched over toward the door of my truck. I asked him if anything was wrong and he replied, "I'm asking Jesus to come into my heart."

It was there, Corbin accepted Christ as his Savior. He was baptized at our church, Pleasant Grove Baptist Church, on July 16, 2000.

∽

Today was no different. I had prayed to God the same prayer I always prayed before Corbin rode, "Win or lose, please God, keep him safe."

The gate flew open and out jumped the bald faced bull with Corbin aboard. Although it was not apparent to me or any of the other on-lookers, the second jump out of the chute was hard and snatched Corbin's hand out of the rope. He was holding on with only two fingers. He knew all he had to do was ride for eight seconds to get a score in order to be in the championship round, so two fingers or all five, he was doing what he had to get the job done.

About five seconds into the ride, Corbin was only holding on to the tail of the rope, still hustling to make the eight seconds. He later told us he had over corrected by shifting his hips too much and the force of the next jump threw him over the bull's head and onto the ground. Before my son could move, the bull had hooked him several times, and spun around with his feet coming down on the back of Corbin's head. The force broke

Corbin's C6 and C7 vertebrae leaving him lying on the arena floor, immediately and totally paralyzed from the chest down.

The wreck with the bull, M33 during the 2008 National High School Finals Rodeo in Farmington, New Mexico

Because of the bright sun, I couldn't see exactly what had happened, but I knew Corbin was lying motionless on the ground, and it was evident to me that he was in trouble. As many bulls as I have seen Corbin ride, I have never seen him hit the

ground and not move except for once
down at the Lazy T. We were bucking out
some practice bulls and my cousin, Darrell
White, had a little Brahman cross bull that
he wanted Corbin to try. Corbin rode the
bull for at least eight seconds, but as he
was trying to jump off, the bull made a
sudden move and threw Corbin into the
iron fence. The right side of his head hit
the fence and for an instant, Corbin was
knocked out. Even then, he was trying
to get up. This is a natural instinct for a
bull rider. Of course, there was no humor
in it at the time, but looking back, we
teased Corbin each time that subject
came up. While Chris Shivers roped the
bull and kept him "choked down" at
the other end of the arena, everyone
ran to Corbin to make sure he was okay.
Eventually, we got him up. I was holding
up fingers to see if he could tell me how
many, but Corbin was more interested
in the bull. He kept saying "th..th...that
bull is ble..blee...bleeding." By this time,
some were giggling, and we assured him
that it wasn't the bull that was bleeding,
it was him! He could see the bull down
at the other end of the arena and was

concerned for his well being, not nearly my main issue at that time! After a few minutes, Corbin was fine and totally back to his senses.

∽

With Corbin still lying motionless, I instructed Colt to stay with some other Louisiana people who were watching while I ran to the arena. I was stopped at the gate by a gentleman who would later become a dear family friend, Tilt James, who is with the Fellowship of Christian Cowboys. Tilt wouldn't allow me to go any further as the paramedics began working on my son. I asked Tilt what was wrong, He assured me Corbin was awake and talking. I knew that wasn't all. Tilt then told me Corbin couldn't move his legs. Call it 'mother's intuition' but I knew it was bad and deep down, I already knew his neck was broken from what Tilt had told me.

I began praying that God would take care of my son like I had seen Him do so many times before. How I wished Dewitt was with us. I knew I had to call him but my fingers simply wouldn't work to press the numbers. I handed my phone to Shane Hood who was by this time standing with Tilt and me. Shane phoned Dewitt.

∽

It was lunch time on the job and Dewitt and the men were taking a break. Dewitt said when he got off of the phone with Shane, he told the other men what had happened then fell to his knees beside his truck and began praying. He told God he knew that He had the power to heal our son but knew it was up to Him if he did it or not. He continued...whatever the outcome, give us strength to accept it.

I was allowed to ride in the ambulance with Corbin to the local hospital, San Juan Regional Medical Center. They immediately took Corbin in for examination. Friends from the rodeo began to gather. The Hoods soon met me in the emergency room and brought Colt.

Standing in the hallway as friends gathered, an ER nurse named Leigh-Anne briefly stopped to talk with me. We immediately had a special bond. From then on, Leigh-Anne came by periodically telling me what they were doing with Corbin. She and several other medical personnel talked to me about the neurosurgeon who was on call that day assuring me that, "Dr. Maurin is one of the top neurosurgeons in the country." I was told this numerous times that day.

What seemed like the longest time passed before they would allow me to see Corbin. When they did, Tilt went into the small room with Colt and me. I was trying my hardest not to cry in front of Corbin, despite the fact that I had been sobbing non-stop since he landed on the ground back at the arena. I walked to him with my hand stretched out, first touching his shoulder.

He said, "Mom, don't touch my shoulder. They said it is broken."

It was then that I noticed the tremendous swelling. As I walked into the room, I was first focused on his eyes, his face and the white neck brace that kept him stable. As long as I live, I will never forget his question. Looking me square in the eye he asked, "Mom will I walk again?"

Though fighting back the tears, I replied, "You bet you are. It's going to take some time and you'll have to have some therapy, but you WILL walk again. Besides, we have half a dozen colts to break when we get home."

At the time, I had no idea if that was a true statement or not. I was simply trying to give Corbin every positive word I could muster. We didn't get to stay with him long that first visit. I knew I couldn't stay and reluctantly left the room when instructed by the nurses to do so.

Sometime later, Dr. Maurin, the neuro-surgeon, came into the tiny room near the ER where we were waiting. He began to tell me that Corbin's C6 and C7 were broken and gave me a "game plan" regarding Corbin's medical treatment.

"First," he said, "I want to place him in traction for a short time. If that doesn't work, I want to take him into surgery this afternoon to repair the vertebrae and get the pressure off of his spinal cord."

Dr. Maurin told us that with an injury like Corbin's, surgery wasn't typically performed for a week or longer to allow time for the swelling to decrease. However, he went on to say that because of Corbin's athletic ability and considering his strength and stamina, he wanted to perform the surgery right away if the traction failed to realign his spinal column.

The only medical experience I have is doctoring a horse or cow from time to time, nothing on a human so I wasn't in a position to argue. I told Dr. Maurin to do whatever he thought was best for my son. I then asked him the question I know he was dreading. I asked, "Will my son walk again?"

Dr. Maurin replied after a short hesitation, "Your son will have a good life. He has a strong upper body and ...."

I interrupted, "What I'm asking is if my son will walk again?"

After a long hesitation, Dr. Maurin answered, "We just don't know what will happen in cases like this."

I knew what Dr. Maurin was trying to tell me. He was trying to say that Corbin would be permanently paralyzed. Colt and I were both sobbing. Once I somewhat regained my composure, I told Dr. Maurin "I know if anyone can do it, Corbin Carpenter can. I know my son and we know the Great Physician."

Minutes later I was told that traction didn't work as hoped to realign Corbin's spinal column and surgery was inevitable. It was to be performed that afternoon as soon as the surgery room was available.

Theresa Freeman Carpenter

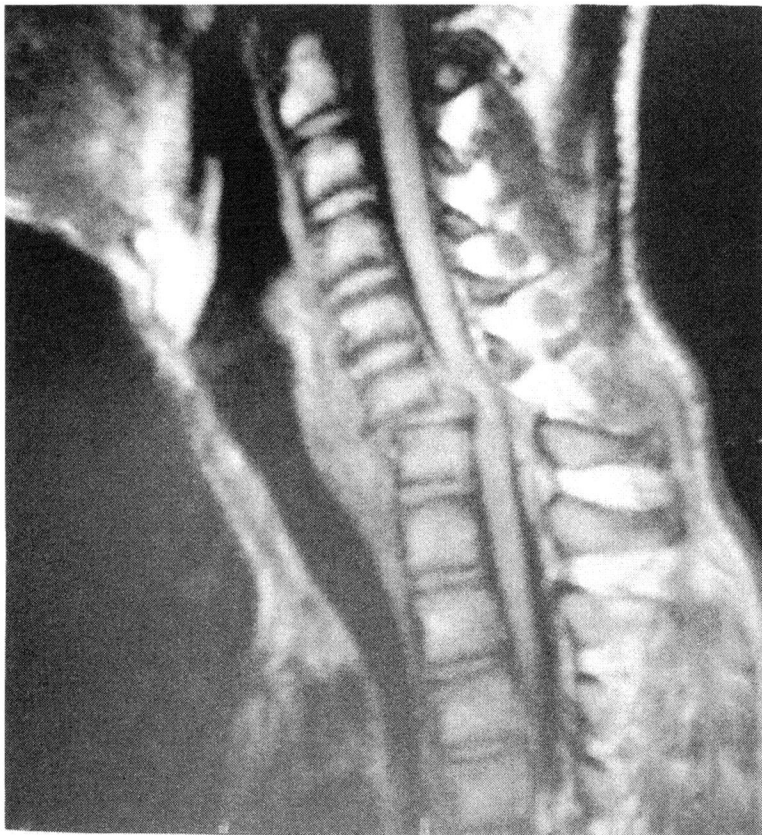

A picture from the MRI, taken on July 25, 2008, showing Corbin's C6 and C7 vertebrae broken as a result from his bull riding injury while competing at the NHSFR in Farmington, NM

(from MRI at San Juan Regional Medical Center)

Back home in Jonesville, many friends and family members were gathering at our home. Dewitt, Courtney and our son-in-law, Roy Wyatt Kemp, were making travel arrangements to get to Farmington. It seemed every avenue of transportation they came up with wouldn't work. That is, until Brian Kennedy made a phone call to a company of which he is affiliated that owned a private jet. Brian was told the jet was in route to Florida and as soon as it landed, the dispatcher would have the pilot call. When the pilot learned of the tragedy, he called Brian, set up a time that afternoon to meet my family in Alexandria, a city which is an hour from our hometown.

Meanwhile, Corbin's surgery went as expected. The vertebrae were repaired but Corbin still could not move at all from his chest down. He was released from post-op later that afternoon and was sent to the room in ICU that would become our home for the next five days. Literally minutes after we were taken into ICU, through the door window of our room and through the one in the main ICU door, I could see people milling around in the waiting room. I knew my family had arrived.

Corbin woke up shortly after Dewitt, Courtney and Wyatt arrived. The first time they talked to Corbin was very emotional for each of us. With calm assurance, Corbin said to his dad, "Dad, don't worry about it. I'm gonna be all right, it ain't nothin' but a thing."

Corbin remained the strongest in our family, never shedding a tear regarding his injury. The only time he wept, was during the wee hours of Sunday morning following the final performance on Saturday night. His bull riding friends were standing bedside, saying their goodbyes as they left the hospital for the last time, headed back to Louisiana and other states. It wasn't until weeks later after Corbin was moved to the Baylor Institute of Rehabilitation in Dallas, Texas, for physical therapy that he revealed to us why he had taken this tragedy so well and felt a peace.

Chapter 4

Despite Corbin's initial surgery, he was experiencing severe pain in his neck. The incision for the first surgery was in the back of his neck. A plate and four screws were secured to his bone to insure stability and to repair the break. However, with the continued pain Corbin was experiencing, Dr. Maurin thought a second surgery, similar to the first, would be helpful to relieve the pain. The second surgery would be on the front of Corbin's neck.

From the beginning of his treatment, pain medication was being administered to Corbin, however, everything they gave him made him nauseated and caused him to frequently throw up. As one can imagine, this was especially difficult being in a neck brace, lying flat on his back. Corbin had never taken any type of pain medication before. As a matter of fact, even as a small child, it was all I could do to get him to take antibiotics, Tylenol, etc. when prescribed by his pediatrician. Following his injury, we soon learned that Corbin could not tolerate morphine, and after several other pain medications were tried, they finally found one that did not make him sick. He didn't like taking any of it and would only agree to do so when the pain was too great.

෮๑

The first surgery was performed on Friday. July 25, 2008, the same day of the accident. Dr. Maurin wanted to do the second surgery the following Monday, July 28th. However, when they started to take Corbin into pre-op, we informed the nurses of the swelling we had noticed in his left arm. They soon realized he had a blood clot in his forearm where the IV had been and the surgery was postponed.

In the meantime, Colt had left the previous Sunday headed back to Louisiana with the Hood family. Courtney and Wyatt were still with us and planned to stay for Corbin's second surgery. However, when it was postponed, because they had left behind their one-year-old daughter, Kaylee, and because of their work, reluctantly they flew home. Corbin was given medication that quickly dissolved the clot and a week later on August 1st, was taken in for the second surgery. It was deemed another successful surgery, immediately relieving the majority of pain in Corbin's neck.

Our friends from Louisiana, Mike and Linda McCartney, happened to be visiting their daughter and her family in a neighboring town to Farmington shortly after Corbin got hurt. They came to be with us during Corbin's second surgery. While waiting for Dr. Maurin in pre-op, Corbin had his usual comedic personality in full swing, and kept our spirits lifted. Because Corbin had to wear a neck brace 24/7, he couldn't reach his neck to scratch when it was itching. Like many in similar situations, he learned to improvise, quickly realizing a plastic dinner knife did the trick. Although Corbin liked and admired Dr. Maurin very much, despite his efforts, Corbin couldn't get him to (in Corbin's words) "lighten up and laugh."

When Dr. Maurin finally walked into the pre-op room prior to the surgery, he asked Corbin, "Well, are you ready to do this?"

Without hesitation, Corbin lifted up that black, plastic dinner knife and said, "Yes sir. I brought my own knife to help you get started."

Dr. Maurin laughed with us for the first time and seemed to have a lighter outlook going forth during our remaining stay at San Juan Regional Medical.

༄

Because Corbin was paralyzed, and unable to move, Dewitt and I had to turn him in his bed periodically from his right side to his left, and vice-versa. The fifth day of our stay at San Juan, while Dewitt and I were turning Corbin, we saw his left leg move. We immediately told the nurses. Some of them rejoiced with us, yet some said he was having muscle spasms. We knew Corbin had moved his leg, and it was nothing short of a miracle. It was the first ray of hope God had shown us that our son had muscle movement.

As I was sitting by Corbin's bedside one afternoon, thinking he was asleep, I ran my finger lightly in a circle around the huge bruise on his upper left thigh. The bruise was the result of the bull stepping on his leg while Corbin was lying motionless on the arena floor after his neck was broken. Corbin's eyes popped open and looking straight upward to the ceiling asked, "You're touching my leg aren't you?"

"Yes" I replied. "What am I doing?"

"You are going around in circles on my thigh," said Corbin.

Tears of joy flowed from both Dewitt and me. Corbin had some feeling despite what we had been told. Each day found slight improvement. We clung to each new thing Corbin was able to do or feel.

The Sunday following Corbin's second surgery which was the ninth day since the incident, Dr. Maurin came in to check our son. He began telling us that everything looked good, and that we would soon be making plans to move Corbin to a rehabilitation center. As he started to leave the room, Dewitt asked, "Wait Doc, didn't they tell you Corbin moved his leg?"

Dr. Maurin replied, "Well, they did tell me something like that. Let's take a look."

We threw back the sheet from Corbin's legs. Dr. Maurin picked up Corbin's left leg underneath his knee and instructed him to kick the ceiling. Well, Corbin didn't kick the ceiling but he did pop his foot up far enough and fast enough that is scared Dr. Maurin so badly that he dropped Corbin's leg, jumped back and said a few choice words!

Dr. Maurin exclaimed, among other things, "We've got to get this boy to rehab fast."

In the beginning as we talked about rehab, Dr. Maurin wanted to send Corbin to the rehab center in Craig, Colorado. However, Chris Shivers had talked to Dr. Tandy Freeman, director of the PBR medial staff, who suggested we bring him to Baylor in Dallas. Baylor is an excellent center and only six hours from home as opposed to the twenty-four or so from Craig.

The following day was Monday, the tenth day of our stay at San Juan. The ladies in the office at the hospital worked diligently to make arrangements to move Corbin the very next morning. Because of his medical needs and distance of travel, he would require a medically equipped airplane for the transfer. At approximately 4:00 p.m. Mountain time in Farmington (6:00 p.m. Central Standard time at home which was after business hours), the hospital representative came into Corbin's room and told me that because of our limited insurance benefits, Baylor would require $26,700.00 in cash to allow Corbin to enter the rehab hospital. My heart sank.

The final day of the National Finals rodeo, a group of Corbin's friends started a 'blue ribbon' campaign in an effort to raise money to help offset the costs of the medical bills. An account had been opened at a local bank in Farmington and donations had been coming in, many from people who were not affiliated with rodeo at all. We had no idea how much money was in the account.

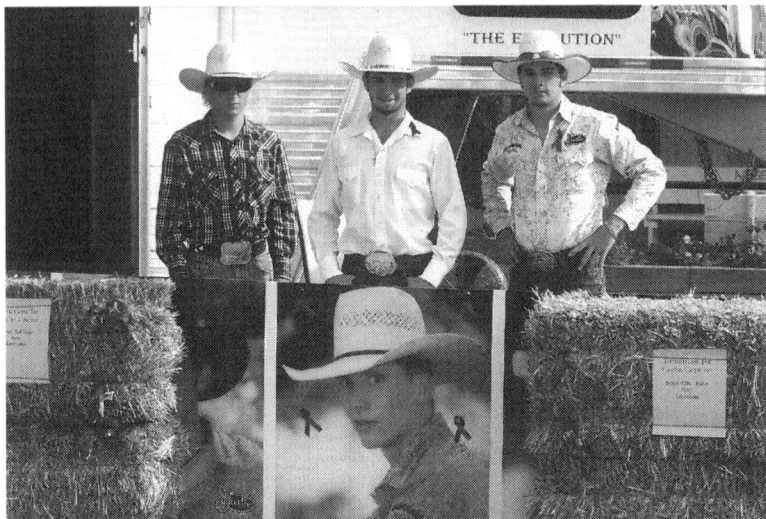

Corey Granger, Colten Blachard, and Shane Hood standing behind Corbin's picture that was displayed at the Bloomer Trailer booth at the 2008 NHSFR. This picture was taken at the beginning of the "Blue Ribbon" Campaign in honor of Corbin. Note the blue ribbons on the cowboys, on the picture, and on the hay.

Dewitt and I agreed that I would fly to Dallas with Corbin the next morning and he would stay behind and go to the bank in Farmington. He would get a Bank Cashiers Check for the funds in the benefit account and I would write a personal check for the difference upon arrival in Dallas. The boys and I had traveled to Farmington in my truck, so once Dewitt went to the bank, he would be on the road headed to Dallas.

Because Dewitt was unfamiliar with Farmington, Tilt James took him to the bank on Tuesday morning when it opened. By this time, Corbin and I were an hour in the air on our way to Dallas. Therefore, I was unable to have any contact with my husband to see how much money was available. We were literally flying out of Farmington on faith that God would provide the funds we needed so our son could be treated.

During the previous ten days following Corbin's injury, people had been coming by the hospital giving us cash and checks to help with the expenses. While the cashier was getting the available balance for Dewitt, he was pulling checks and cash out of his wallet to be added to the total in the account. When Dewitt turned around, there were two, one-hundred dollar bills lying on the counter that he hadn't placed there. He knew Tilt had laid them down.

Dewitt said, "Tilt, you don't have to do that, you've done more than enough to help us already."

Tilt replied, "You are not going to cheat me out of my part of this blessing."

The money stayed.

We had to have $26,700 in order for Baylor to accept Corbin. Once all of the funds were totaled, there was $26,800. Dewitt told the lady at the bank to cut a check for the entire amount, apparently Baylor needed it worse than we did. Dewitt would be bringing the check with him when he arrived that night. God is so good!

Corbin and I landed at the airport in Dallas and were taken to Baylor by an awaiting ambulance. It wasn't until he was rolled off of the fourth floor elevator at Baylor that the personnel at the nurse's station told us they had received a faxed copy of the Bank Cashiers Check for the full amount. We were good to go. God had answered many prayers that were sent up on our behalf. He wasn't going to stop that day.

Chapter 5

Upon our arrival at Baylor, Corbin was assigned a team of therapists. Dr. Rita Hamilton had accepted Corbin's case prior to our arrival and would head up the team. The first day was spent with each member of the team individually coming into Corbin's room to become acquainted with him. In the process, they each asked questions. Ryan, his physical therapist, asked Corbin what his expectations were upon leaving Baylor. To that, Corbin replied, "I'm walking out of here."

Ryan then asked him what his long term goals were. Corbin told him he was going to be 100% and was going to ride bulls again. Ryan commented on what a good attitude Corbin had but it was obvious that he thought Corbin was being unrealistic about his expectations. Afterall, he had broken his C6 and C7 vertebra pinching his spinal cord. Medically speaking, the outcome of that type injury pretty much spoke for itself.

∾

By the time Corbin reached Baylor, he was still only able to move his left leg and left toes. Ryan told us they would work with whatever muscles he had on any given day. Still, from all medical personnel involved, we were given little hope of even partial recovery.

Rehabilitation proved to be hard, one of the hardest things Corbin said he had ever done. He commented several times that he had never worked so hard for such a small amount of progress. He said that loading, unloading and stacking one thousand square bales of hay by himself wouldn't be as hard as the work he faced in rehab. However, Corbin took on the task of rehabilitation with great dedication and direction. If he were instructed to do ten repetitions of a certain exercise, as hard as he found it to be, he would do fifteen, never complaining. His positive attitude remained unwavered, and he was willing and determined to do whatever it took to be able to once again rodeo.

Each day found Corbin a little stronger. He was still on numerous medications, something very unfamiliar to him to say the least. Many times he would get nauseated and vomit during a therapy session. He wiped his mouth and said "All right, let's go again."

Marrisa, Corbin's occupational therapist, said in all of her years of working with patients, she had never seen anyone with such determination and grit. She commented to us that many times she has witnessed patients get sick in the same manner, give up and go to their room for the rest of the day. Not Corbin. He was ready to do it again.

One day, Corbin was extremely nauseated, and in general, not feeling well. Much to our surprise, that night Corbin passed a huge kidney stone the size of a grain of rice. A half hour later, he was feeling fine and the next morning, ready for another hard day of work.

"The faster I can walk out of here," he said, "the faster I can go back to rodeoing." It was that mentality that kept him motivated.

∽

While we had been at Baylor, we noticed a standing device in the work out area that one could be strapped into, and the seat would slowly rise until the person was in a standing position. Corbin had been in rehab for about four weeks when he asked Ryan when he would put him into one of those devices. The following day Ryan agreed. However, when they tried to stand Corbin, his blood pressure dropped, and they would not allow him to go any higher for fear he would faint. We were very disappointed to say the least but none more so than Corbin. For the next three days, we experienced the same disappointment. Finally, they wrapped Corbin's legs with large "Ace" bandages in an effort to maintain a high enough blood pressure that would allow him to stand. It was a success. Although we knew Corbin wasn't standing totally under his own power, we were very proud and it gave us even more hope. This was the first time we had seen our son in a standing position in about six weeks.

At Baylor, a psychologist is on the team assigned to each patient. The lady assigned to Corbin's team came by to visit him at least on a weekly basis beginning the first day of our arrival. She explained to Dewitt and me upon her initial visit with Corbin that he seemed to be accepting his injury and the circumstances well. She went on to say that although he was presently doing fine, he would eventually become depressed and need some professional guidance. About her fourth visit with Corbin, she exited his room shaking her head. She told Dewitt and me that in all of her years of counseling trauma patients, she had never seen one that didn't eventually go through depression and/or anger... until now, that is. She found Corbin's attitude quite amazing and even suggested he visit with other patients in an effort to lift their spirits. What she didn't know is that once therapy sessions ended each day, Corbin already spent many afternoons visiting other patients on the spinal cord injury floor (SCI).

There were several fellow patients on our floor who were about Corbin's age. Each floor of Baylor had a kitchen area available to the patients and almost every afternoon Corbin would request one of his favorite snacks, pop corn. Most visits he would make to other patients included him taking a freshly popped bag of pop corn to share. He took advantage of his visits to share his testimony and explain to them how God was seeing him through the ordeal. He told them that he looked to God for strength and they could, too. He also encouraged them to put forth 110% during their rehab sessions, and reassured them the therapists were there to help them. Some of these guys were experiencing major depression, and anger. Corbin tried to help. He wanted them to feel good about themselves despite their new limitations.

∽

As Dewitt and Corbin were returning from a therapy session one afternoon, Corbin told his dad that he thought he finally had Ryan going his way.

He went on to say, "I knew Ryan didn't believe me that first day when I told him I was walking out of here, but I think he's comin' around to it now." Corbin continued, "I never thought I would stay in a wheelchair for the rest of my life. While I was lying on the arena floor, God spoke to me. He told me just as plain as I can hear you, that I would be all right. He gave me a peace."

It was at this point that we finally realized why Corbin had accepted his injury so well and the results thereof. We knew then why he was never depressed or angry. God had given our son all of the assurance he needed to get through the rough times he faced and the strength to press forward. Praise God for His love and mercy!

∞

Dewitt and I seldom left Corbin's side the entire time he was in the hospital both at San Juan and Baylor. Although God had provided many people to keep our businesses back home on track, periodically Dewitt would return home. Perhaps the most important reason to return home was to be with Colt, who by this time was back in school.

By the last week of August, Hurricane Gustov was creating quite a disturbance in the Gulf of Mexico. Its projected path would put it ashore in Louisiana. With Wyatt, our son-in-law, being off shore at work, Dewitt decided he needed to be at home with Courtney and Colt in the event central Louisiana was affected. Sure enough, on August 31, 2008, Hurricane Gustov came ashore in south Louisiana dropping torrential rainfall from east Texas to west Mississippi. On September 1, it had reached central Louisiana leaving behind twenty plus inches of rainfall flooding many homes and businesses. Although both our home and Wyatt and Courtney's home were spared, our business was not. As I was having lunch with my friend, Cindy Emmons, from Fairfield, Texas, on a rare occasion of leaving the hospital, Dewitt called to share the news. I knew this was a call he was not looking forward to. In our farm equipment dealership/western store, we had six inches of water standing and lost over $11,000 of merchandise. Although the store was a mess and cleanup was not easy, this was nothing in comparison to what we were experiencing with our child. We had lost only material things; no one was injured. God sure has a way of putting things into perspective.

After several days of Corbin standing in the device known as a 'standing frame,' Ryan promoted him to a rolling device called a Lite Gait. The Lite Gate came about chest high to him and allowed him to rest his arms on top for balance. It had a parachute harness type support between his legs which only allowed, at first, about 30% of his body weight to be on his legs. I cannot express the joy we felt the first time we saw our son take a step. We knew, of course, that he wasn't doing it on his own, but it was a miracle especially since we were told he would never walk again. I snapped pictures as Corbin would humbly say, "It's really not a big deal, I told y'all I was gonna do this." Again, Corbin's determination had not wavered.

This walking ritual continued for several days. Corbin's left side remained strongest and his right foot dragged somewhat, especially when he was tired. Either Ryan or Marrissa would sometimes help him move his right foot when taking steps. With this, we could see even his right side getting stronger almost daily.

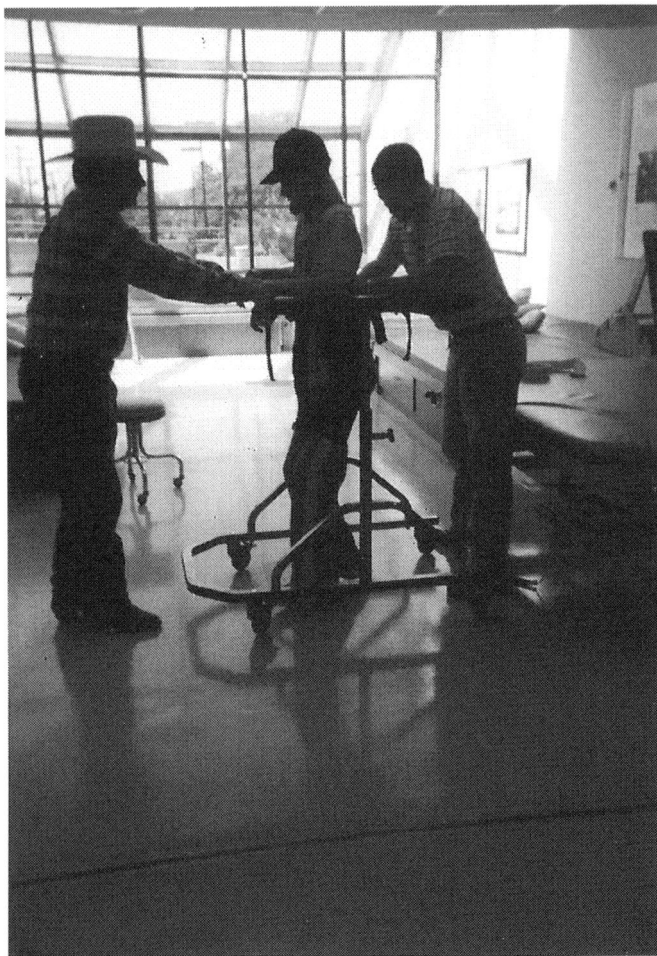

Corbin learning to walk again with help of the Lite Gait. Assisting him in the process was his dad, in front, and his physical therapist, Ryan, in back.

After several days on the Lite Gait, Corbin graduated to a treadmill, still with a harness to help support his body weight. Each day, he gradually grew stronger and was carrying more of his own weight on his legs. Eventually he was walking with a walker then finally, Corbin was allowed to participate in Aquatic therapy. We quickly saw a vast improvement; though far from being as strong as he had been prior to the accident, his strength and stamina were quickly increasing.

Corbin taking an Aquatic therapy class, during his final days of rehab at Baylor.

It was indicated to us that Corbin would be discharged at the end of week following his fifth week of rehab, a date we had all been looking forward to. However, as the time approached, Corbin showed such drastic improvement that Ryan wanted him to stay an additional week. Reluctantly, Corbin agreed.

The following week passed slowly for us as we had all been away from home too long. Corbin made it very plain to each involved that he would stay one more week but not to ask for another. He said it was time to see the Bar CC Ranch and his own bed! Including the time Corbin had been gone to help Chris and Mike at the bull riding school, the IFYR rodeo in Shawnee, Oklahoma, the NHSFR and now rehab, in all, Corbin had been away from home for about four months. This was far longer than he had ever been gone before.

During our final week at Baylor, Corbin was moved from the corner room that had become our "home away from home" for the previous five plus weeks to a room at the opposite end of the building, still on the fourth floor. Our new room was called a "transition room" and was frequently occupied by those about to leave Baylor and go home. It was set up more like a home setting with a normal bed verses a hospital type bed, a regular chest of drawers, etc. The purpose of the transition room was to see how patients would handle a home setting rather than a hospital setting with all of the normal conveniences. As caregivers, Dewitt and I were to administer Corbin's medications and perform all of the necessary duties that he would require once we arrived at home. After having taken up residence in our previous room for well over a month, we had lots of items to move from one end of the building to the other. Many people had brought gifts, food, etc. that had to be relocated. It took several trips with rolling carts piled high to get all of our belongings moved to the transition room.

Each of the rooms was set up to accommodate the patient plus one caregiver or family member. This means there was typically only one chair in each room that unfolded into a bed. Since Dewitt and I both had stayed with Corbin the majority of the time, the nurses "sneaked" an extra roll out chair into our room. We realized on the first trip to the transition room that there was only one chair so we decided to move the second. Dewitt began pushing it as Corbin wheeled along beside him. My husband can be quite the motivator which was evidenced by the way he pushed Corbin during his workouts. Dewitt quickly came to the conclusion that Corbin would get an extra exercise session if he pushed the chair with his wheelchair and so he did. By the time he reached the opposite end of the hallway, Corbin was exhausted but had accomplished yet another feat!

We had been residents of the transition room for only a few days when professional bull rider and friend, Mike White, came to visit. Mike had been to a bull riding that weekend and had flown into Dallas to pickup his truck. While Mike was in the room with us, we noticed Corbin wasn't acting like himself. He, Mike and Chris usually tease each other unmercifully but this particular day found him very quiet and reserved. Chris, Corbin and Mike, when in Jonesville, along with other friends, typically roped at Chris' at least once or twice during each week. Following the ropings, Chris and Corbin would be found wrestling in the dirt in the middle of the arena. Because neither had an ounce of "give up" to their name, the contest could go on forever! Courtney was at one of the ropings when the "tussling broke out." She asked friend Lee White how long they keep that up? To that, Lee said, "Who could say? This could go on for hours."

♋

When Mike began to leave from his visit, we asked Corbin if he wanted to go down with him on the elevator but he declined. It wasn't until later that night we learned why. Corbin passed yet another large kidney stone. Not one to complain, he later commented that the only time he was glad his feeling was impaired was while he had the two kidney stones!

♋

While Corbin was hospitalized, I only returned home twice. Once only overnight so Dewitt and I could attend business and

84

make arrangements for our lengthy stay away from home and our businesses. The second time was for a weekend to attend a benefit rodeo in our hometown that was held in Corbin's honor. While we were gone, our longtime friends Christi and Greg Deason came to Dallas to be with Corbin.

The proceeds from the rodeo would be used to help pay for Corbin's medical expenses, and the event was tremendous! Hundreds of people turned out to support our family. Our friend, Bill Brown, served as the announcer and was able to reach Corbin by cell phone during the performance. He held the phone to the microphone which gave Corbin an opportunity to thank the crowd for their support. Everyone stood and cheered. It was emotional for all.

When we returned to Baylor on Sunday afternoon, Greg told us he had taken Corbin for a "stroll" around the block. It had rained the night before and there were a few small puddles left behind. Greg pushed Corbin's wheelchair into a small, muddy area making it hard to push it out. As always, Corbin's sense of humor was intact. He said, "Mr. Greg, I believe you're gonna have to put this buggy in four wheel drive to get us out!"

One of Corbin's best friends, Slade Deason, who is Christi and Greg's son, came to Baylor to visit on several occasions. Toward the end of Corbin's stay, he brought with him a roping dummy which is a roughly simulated figure of a steer used for roping practice. The boys drew quite the audience on the second floor veranda as they swung and caught. Corbin didn't have good use of his right arm at that time but did manage to throw a few side loops. It was the closest thing to normal Corbin had experienced in several months and it sure made him happy.

Chapter 6

On September 26, 2008, Corbin was finally discharged. He fulfilled the promise he made the first day we arrived. With the help of his dad, he WALKED out of Baylor. It was only two days away from Courtney's twenty-fifth birthday, and what a great gift it was to her, to us all!

In 2004, the same year Courtney and Wyatt were married, we had built a mother-in-law's suite on to our house for my husband's mom. Sadly, she passed away suddenly after only living there for a few months. The main part of our home is three feet off the ground, and the suite is at ground level. I thought it would be convenient for Corbin to stay downstairs for a while, at least until he gained the strength to move up and down the steps on his own. He had other plans. I didn't even get the suggestion out of my mouth good when he told me it was "business as usual" around there. He was sleeping in his own bed. That he did.

The Saturday following our return home, a couple of Corbin's buddies took him for a ride. Little did he know, over one-hundred family members and friends were gathering at our house for a surprise welcome home party. When the boys were nearing our house, Corbin saw all of the vehicles. He couldn't imagine why all of those folks were there, it never occurred to him they were gathering for him. For many of the folks present, it was the first time they had seen Corbin since he left in the summer. He was overwhelmed!

It was fall, and dove season was in full swing. Corbin was not yet strong enough to get to his favorite hunting spot. However, he was able to convince his younger brother, Colt, to push him around our yard and the pasture at our house in his wheelchair so he could shoot a few doves. The hunt was successful! Both Corbin and Colt had a blast. The memories made from that hunt will forever stand out in Colt's mind.

Two weeks after our return home from Baylor, anxious to ride again, Corbin asked his dad to put him on his little roping mare, Pud. His balance, though exceptional prior to the accident, had not yet been reestablished. Not only did Corbin miss riding, he felt it would be instrumental in helping regain his balance and stamina. By this time, he had begun taking physical therapy in Jonesville under father/daughter team, Tom and Summer Miliken three times weekly. He continued pushing himself, and in the months that followed, therapy became difficult, not to Corbin this time, but to Summer. He had progressed so quickly, that she found herself unable to develop enough 'hurdles' that would challenge him!

Theresa Freeman Carpenter

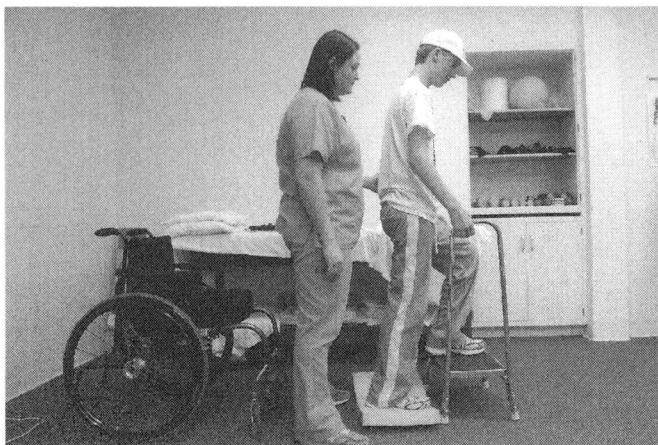

Corbin taking instruction from Summer Milliken
at Miss-Lou Physical therapy in Jonesville
(photo courtesy of Liz Condo)

Working out in our game room at home
(photo courtesy of Liz Condo)

Slade Deason was visiting (our house was his second home, one might say), when he and Corbin decided to go riding. Corbin asked Slade to push him up on Pud. Slade gave a little boost but not hard enough to get Corbin to the saddle.

Corbin said, "Come on man, push harder."

Slade gave a big push, pushing Corbin up and over the saddle, and onto the ground. Corbin began laughing. He said he didn't know which was the funniest, falling to the ground, or the look on Slade's face!

Finally, Corbin said, "Man, you pushed a little too hard that time."

∽

It was October 31, 2008, just over a month since we had been home. For the first time since Corbin was injured, several people had gathered at our home to rope steers. Prior to him leaving in the summer, like at Chris', a group regularly came to our place to rope calves and steers.

Dewitt saddled Pud, led her to the roping pen, tied her, and left her standing. Corbin was sitting in his wheelchair in the roping pen. By this time, he could stand up on his own, and take a few steps holding onto something or someone. He rolled his wheelchair to Pud, stood up, made his way to her side, and literally "climbed" on by himself. Although he was still unable to rope, he managed to push steers out of the roping pen. When he finished riding, he dismounted Pud totally unassisted. He soon realized he was too far from his wheelchair to get there by himself. Determined to do it alone, Pud lowered her head, and Corbin slipped his arm over her neck.

He said to her, "Let's go."

Slowly, Pud helped Corbin to his wheelchair, and lowered her head further as he sat down. The bond between those two has always been unbelievable!

∾

As time passed, Corbin was growing stronger each day, and eventually was walking using only a walking cane. It was not just any cane, but one that family friend, Bill Brown, had made for him. Corbin's name was burned into the wood, and the handle was made from a deer antler. Corbin said if he had to use a cane, he at least wanted one that looked cool, and he wanted "Uncle Bill" to make it for him.

By now, we were being asked to share our testimony at various churches and organizations of how God was healing Corbin. This particular Sunday, we were speaking at Utility Baptist Church, a church that my family and I attended when I was a child. After speaking at Utility that day, we returned home, and Corbin laid his walking cane down to eat lunch. He never picked it up again.

By Christmas of 2008, only five months after Corbin's injury, he could saddle his horse without assistance, and was riding daily. Many of these days taking advantage of the piece of hunting property we own that is located near our house. We regularly ride horses on this four hundred plus acre property, and it has proven an excellent place to "put some wet saddle blankets" on young horses, or simply take a relaxing ride. Corbin and Colt ride the perimeters almost daily, and if a horse needs a really good workout, riding through the sloughs and ditches can quickly take the edge off of one, or get one into shape. One particular day, there was a group of us, maybe eight or so people riding this property we refer to as "Daggett." Corbin was riding Pud. He and a couple of his friends rode ahead of us, and Dewitt and I rejoiced as we watched him lope up, back Pud up, spin her around, then do it again. That was the old Corbin showing up! How we had prayed to see that again!

გ

We closed the year 2008 with an awesome trip to a wild game ranch near Carthage, Texas. While Corbin was in San Juan Regional Medical Center, we were visited by a family who owned the ranch but were living in Farmington at the time. They invited Corbin to come to the ranch when he was feeling better, and had called prior to Christmas to set the date. The plan was for us to leave Jonesville a few days after Christmas to meet them on the ranch. However, due to illness in their family, they were unable to be with us but had a guide lined up to show us the place in their absence. There were a couple of Axis deer that needed harvesting so Corbin was allowed to take one! The mounted Axis along with a great picture is now hanging in our home to remind us of the awesome time we had. PRCA Professional cowboy, Tildon Hooper, a cousin to the land owners, came to spend the day with us. He and Corbin quickly found they had a lot in common, and instantly made friends.

Theresa Freeman Carpenter

Corbin harvested this Axis deer on an exotic game ranch near Carthage, Texas (Left to right) our hunting guide, Corbin, Tildon Hooper, and Colt. December 2008

Chapter 7

God had continually blessed us throughout this ordeal. He was constantly showing us the way, and opening doors for Corbin that we thought had been closed forever. One day short of seven months after the accident, Corbin backed Pud into the roping box in our practice pen, and he came out roping. His first competition was almost two months later on April 21, 2009 at Chris Shivers' pen. In Corbin's words, "It didn't turn out too good." Then on April 24, 2009, just one day short of nine months since he was injured, Corbin won two team ropings back to back, one of them with his faithful buddy, Slade Deason.

By late spring 2009, Corbin decided he was riding well enough to again accept outside horses. The first horse he accepted simply needed riding and training so with this, Corbin was back in business. A month later, he took in another horse, a palomino gelding that he had ridden before he had gotten hurt. However, for whatever reason the horse had since developed some bad habits. It had been a year or more prior when Corbin first rode this gelding, and when he left our place, didn't have any buck left in him. But apparently the little palomino found it again somewhere along the way, and dumped Corbin. Of all places, Corbin landed on his head! So I am told, he got back on, and rode the horse out. To my knowledge, that was the only time the horse bucked while Corbin had him the second time. It wasn't until several months later that Corbin and his friend, Ethan House, told me this story!

All along, I knew Corbin would eventually get back on bulls. It had been his drive the entire time he was going through therapy, and believed God had it in His plan. Dewitt and I really didn't care about him riding again, but knew it was inevitable. We have always supported our children in whatever they wanted to do, and Corbin riding bulls again would be no different. I told him that if he decided to ride again, I would be the one videoing, and I would be cheering the loudest. Likewise, his dad would be there to pull his rope. We have always placed our children in God's care. This would be no different.

Each time Corbin would go to Chris' arena when they were bucking bulls, I would think to myself, "This is it, he'll come home and tell us he got on one tonight." I would always pay close attention to whether or not he left the house with his riggin' bag, however, this would not be an indication at all. Corbin had always ridden with his right hand, but had decided to start back trying to ride with his left hand since that side remained strongest, and the least affected by his injury. Chris rides left handed, and agreed to help Corbin make the switch.

Little did we know, in early summer 2009, Slade, Colt and Corbin were at our barn where there were a few small bulls penned. They loaded them up, and Corbin got on. From this, Corbin realized he was not yet strong enough to compete on the tough ones. However, he was not discouraged at all from his dream of riding again. Perhaps a little aggravated best described his feelings. His heart and mind were ready to ride again, his body was not. He worked out even harder in an effort to regain the needed strength and balance.

∾

The summer rodeos of 2009 were approaching, and it was obvious that Corbin was upset that he wouldn't be able to compete in the two largest youth rodeos in the country. It was his decision not to attend school during the 2008-09 school year so he could focus on his rehabilitation. It wasn't that he wasn't able to go to school, but his intention was to get back in shape so he could finish his senior year high school rodeoing. Because he was not registered as a student, he would not be eligible to compete at the National Finals High School Rodeo (NFHSR) nor at the International Finals Youth Rodeo (IFYR) in Shawnee, OK. One of his main concerns, however, was that he wouldn't be asked to be a part of the Bloomer Trailer Team again because he wasn't riding, and felt he couldn't contribute to the team. The Bloomers take great pride in selecting their high school team members. They go to great strides selecting the "cream of the crop" among high school cowboys and cowgirls. Not only do they want the best competitors in the events, but they chose those who have notable leadership abilities, good character and morals as well as outgoing personalities. They want students who they will be proud to have represent their company. One can imagine Corbin's excitement when he received a phone call from Randy Bloomer early in 2009. Not only did Randy ask Corbin to be a member, but he was named Team Captain. What an honor!

With that, Easter weekend found us in Salado, Texas at the Bloomer Team meeting. As before, it was a great weekend with the Bloomer family and other team members. World Champion Bull Rider, Tuff Hedeman, and Pro Rodeo Hall of Fame Announcer Pam Minick were there along with professional cowboy, Josh Peek, and other guests. These professionals were on hand to lend advice to the young cowboys and cowgirls who were now Bloomer Team members. We didn't know when we arrived that Corbin was going to be seated at the head table among the guests, and would have a part in the program. By now, we had been traveling to many places giving our testimonies so public speaking had become second nature to Corbin, unlike at the age of four holding his "notes" while reciting his speech at the JBBA national convention. Pam remembered well interviewing Corbin the prior year. She teased him because he had been so nervous talking to her then. Not only had she remembered, but the returning team members and their families remembered as well. We all laughed.

Corbin had gotten to know Tuff Hedeman over the past couple of years as his son, Lane, had been a member of the Bloomer Team in 2008. Also, Tuff had visited Corbin twice while he was in Baylor. He had some very kind words to say on Corbin's behalf. Among other things, Tuff said when he first saw Corbin lying in that bed at Baylor, he thought the kid was finished. He left the room, and cried.

༄

A few months passed, and it was time to attend the IFYR and NHSFR. By now, Corbin had been featured on the cover of several magazines including *NHSRA Times* (July 2009 issue) in an article entitled "Standing Tall." Also, owner/editor, Siri Stevens, featured him in the May 2009 issue of *Rodeo News* where his picture coming off of the bull M33 at the finals a year earlier was on the front cover. In May 2009, Susie McIntyre asked Corbin to be guest speaker giving his testimony at the Championship Timed Events in Guthrie, Oklahoma during a filmed episode of Cowboy Church. The episode has since been aired on RFD-TV several times, and an excerpt from his testimony was included in a Cowboy Church broadcast of Christian bull riders of the PBR. Corbin had also been in numerous other magazines, news stories, and had made several other television appearances. He was always very humble with his new found popularity. He never realized that his outgoing personality, his faithfulness to God, and the fact that he never wanted to bring attention to himself were the very reasons he was so respected. He knew God performed miracles everyday. He trusted in what God told him as he lay on the arena floor that day, and knew he would be all right. It never occurred to him what the big deal was.

He often said, "Some cowboys get broken arms, some get broken legs, I got a broke neck. Big deal, things like that happen. I'll ride bulls again, that's just what I do."

As I think about all of the magazines and newspapers Corbin has been in, and the interviews he has done through the past years, I can't help thinking back to the first time his picture appeared in a magazine when he was about fourteen-years-old. There was a monthly sports magazine based out of Alexandria, Louisiana, and the editor had been by our store several times wanting my advertising business. In each issue, Chris Shivers' stats, PBR standings, etc. was printed, and I had sponsored the page. Knowing we were friends with Chris, he asked me what the chances were of getting Corbin, Dewitt, and more importantly, Chris, to go on a hog hunting trip if he were to arrange one. The editor wanted to have an exclusive story about Chris. Loving hog hunting as much as they do, all agreed to go. A few weeks passed following the hunt when the editor came into the store, excitedly sharing with me the awesome experience. He said he had made lots of wonderful pictures, and what a great article it would be in his magazine. He went on to say he had some really good pictures of 'Conrad.' Although I had no idea who Conrad was, I just smiled, and shook my head, assuming it was someone else who had gone along for the ride. When the next month's issue came out, there was a great picture of Corbin leaned against a horse trailer and the caption underneath read "Conrad Carpenter." We teased Corbin unmercifully. Several of our friends continued calling him that; namely, Joe Higdon, Darrell White, and one of Corbin's best friends, Colter White.

Chapter 8

Like the year prior, because of a dirt contract that had just started, Dewitt couldn't make the trip to the IFYR and NHSFR with us so Corbin, Colt , and I headed out with travel trailer in tow. My first book, *Spurs, Chaps and Faith: The Corbin Carpenter Story* had been published in late June 2009 so we had several hundred copies with us for book signings and speaking engagements that were scheduled. Corbin and I were to speak at several places in both Shawnee, and back in Farmington at the NHSFR. We were hoping our book sales would be successful as the proceeds would be used to help pay the remaining medical bills Corbin incurred the year before.

Only a couple of weeks before we left for the summer rodeos, Colt had managed to break the growth plate in his left ankle. Of all of the calves, steers and junior bulls he had been on, of all of the horses he has ridden, and cows we have penned and worked, it was a bicycle accident that broke his ankle! It was just before dark in early July. Seldom do any of us get in the house before dark, but this particular night was an exception. I had already cooked supper, and was waiting for the boys to come in to serve it. Dewitt and I had just sat down, and turned our television to a good western movie when I heard a moaning sound in the distance. Dewitt and I looked curiously at each other. I decided to get up and look outside. I could see Colt crawling from the driveway toward the house. When we took him to the doctor, sure enough, the growth plate was broken. He spent the rest of the summer on crutches. That's what ramping a culvert on a bicycle will get you!

Jake Hebert, Corbin's good friend and fellow rough stock rider from Louisiana, was also a member of the Bloomer Team that year. His mom, Lisa, and I hosted a "Louisiana" night for the Bloomer Team members and their families. Everyone enjoyed the southern cooking we provided, and gift bags of Cajun goodies were delivered to each team member. When the last barrel was run, and the final bull bucked out, the Bloomer Trailer Team had an outstanding rodeo, and was named the high point team of the 2009 IFYR!

On Friday, the day before the IFYR championship round, the boys and I left Shawnee headed to Farmington, a town and people we had become so familiar with just one short year prior. We had ten speaking engagements scheduled in about eight days, beginning with Sunday's Cowboy Church hosted by the Fellowship of Christian Cowboys, and none other than Tilt James. It was wonderful to see Tilt again, and as a bonus, a couple of our nurses from San Juan Regional Medical Center came to hear us speak. As soon as we spoke at Cowboy Church, the boys and I had to leave for another speaking engagement during the morning service at the Bloomfield First Baptist Church. It was not until later that week that we were actually able to visit with our nurse friends, Leigh-Anne, Melanie and others.

When we left San Juan Regional Medical Center the year before, Corbin made a promise. He said he would return for the 2009 NHSFR and WALK into the arena. The 2009 NHSFR was opened with Corbin not walking into the arena, he did better than that...he RODE a horse around the arena tipping his hat to the crowd! He received a standing ovation. Little did we know, it had been arranged for Corbin's neurosurgeon, Dr. Maurin, to make a surprise appearance to welcome Corbin into the arena. However, there was a miscommunication so it didn't happen. Dr. Maurin was present, but the miscommunication was the location he was supposed to enter into the arena. It wasn't until several days later that we were able to visit with Dr. Maurin. At that time, we learned of the surprise.

We had a great visit with Dr. Maurin. When he asked Corbin what his plans were, he added, "Don't tell me you're going to ride bulls again?"

Corbin smiled that big smile, and simply said, "Yes sir, that's the plan."

Dr. Maurin was not surprised, and added that he knew that was Corbin's driving force all along. He also told him that he may break his neck in another place, but with the plates and screws he had in him now, that area was stronger than it ever was before the accident. Corbin reminded us of that each time in the future he would talk about riding bulls again.

Dr. Maurin and Corbin during our 2009 return visit to the NHSFR in Farmington, NM

111

༄

The volunteers who were so devoted to making the NHSFR a success, had a table set up for my books next to the main entrance door of the rodeo trade show. I set up for several hours each day to sell my books, *Spurs, Chaps and Faith: The Corbin Carpenter Story*, but Corbin was harder to "lasso" in to stay in one spot. I would usually have him autograph books each night for those who asked for it during the day. Corbin being on the front cover of the *NHSRA Times* magazines that were floating around the rodeo assisted in making our story known. Book sells were great, and the funds generated by them went a long way toward paying Corbin's medical bills.

One of the highlights of our trip was the invitation we accepted from the Calvin Yazzi family to tour the Navajo Indian Reservation, and surrounding areas of Kirtland, New Mexico. Calvin's wife, Neva, prepared a picnic lunch for us before we set out for a day of touring and history lesson. The boys and I found it very exciting, and each of us asked many questions. It was again with regret that Dewitt wasn't with us, he would have enjoyed it so. We got to know Calvin and his family when Corbin was in the hospital a year prior. Being a Christian family, they felt God had lead them to Corbin's hospital room. We have stayed in contact with them since that time, and they have sent us many awesome handmade gifts that we will forever treasure.

We met so many people when we returned to Farmington. One young man's mom emailed me shortly after our return home saying how much her "sheep rider" son enjoyed Corbin's short visit with him. She said her son was about to start riding calves, and asked Corbin for advice because he always got butterflies in his stomach thinking about getting on one. According to this young cowboy's mom, Corbin told him not to give up, and to always pray before he got on. He told the young man he got butterflies, too, and praying always helped him.

Our days in the Four Corners area of New Mexico were busy ones. Among the numerous speaking engagements that were scheduled, radio stations began calling, asking us for live interviews. We accepted as many as we could during our week in Farmington. However, we soon found that time wouldn't allow us to do them all, and began turning down offers to appear toward the end of the week. We had been gone from home well over two weeks, and wanted to 'caravan' home with friends so the boys and I wouldn't be traveling the long distance alone. When Friday came, one day before the final performance, we said our good-byes and thank yous and were bound for the Bar CC.

Like a lot of rodeos, the kids spend many hours at night following the rodeo performance, sitting on the tailgates of trucks, playing guitars, singing, and visiting. Like our state finals, they had done this almost every night during the national finals. On our way home, Corbin told me the sweetest story. He said that one night while we were in Farmington, he and

Jake Hebert were sitting on a tailgate playing guitars, and singing. Corbin and the National High School Rodeo Queen, Taci Shaffer from Utah, had been talking since they met shortly after our arrival in Farmington. I, too, met Taci, and she is a beautiful young lady with an awesome personality. This particular night, Corbin asked Jake to play and sing a song they had written together, while he asked Taci to dance. I thought that was the sweetest thing ever when Corbin told me. Kallan Mudd remembered this vividly, and made reference to it in an article she wrote in the October 15, 2010 issue of *Rodeo News* magazine.

Corbin, Taci Shaffer, and Jake Hebert playing
guitars after one of the night performances
of the National Finals High School Rodeo.
July 2009

Chapter 9

After we returned home from the summer rodeos, Corbin continued his bi-weekly physical therapy, that is, when he felt it was convenient to go. If a cow-penning or roping came up, for example, then, in his eyes, therapy wasn't necessary for that day. He felt he had a good workout doing whatever activity he was doing that particular day. I'm sure he was right.

Colt was getting ready to start rodeoing in junior high, and as Corbin coached him calf roping, he, too, would sometimes practice. He was mainly break away or knot roping, and often tying them, too. Despite our encouragement for Corbin to rope at the high school rodeos, he still felt he was too slow to dismount, get to the calf, tie, and have a competitive run. Corbin never, in any circumstance, wanted to bring attention to himself. He practiced with Colt, and coached him regularly. Dewitt and I could see the improvement in both of our boys, but Corbin would never agree to allow me to enter him once high school rodeos started again. He feared he would have a bad run, and people would say something like, "Well, at least he's trying." He never wanted to be any different than anyone else competing.

During his senior year, 2009-10, Corbin was team roping with his good friend from the Deville, Louisiana area, Collin Cammack. Collin headed for Corbin and they put together some good runs through the year. The trophy belt buckles they received after winning the high school rodeo in Gonzales, Louisiana, proved to be the first award belt buckle Collin had ever won! They were both very proud!

Corbin and Collin Cammack team roping during
the 2009-10 high school rodeo season.

◌◊◌

Shortly after Dewitt and I married, we
bought a Catahoula King mare (goes back
to King P234) that was bred to Docs Sug,
one of the hottest going cutting horse sires
of the 1980's. The colt, named Docahoula
by our oldest son, Lee, was a nice little
black stallion that we had had trained to
cut, and we had him on the show circuit.
Unfortunately, he was struck by lightening
while standing in my dad's pasture during

119

an unexpected thunder storm. Since the bottom had fallen out of farming, we didn't feel we could afford to get back into the cutting horse business at that time, however, continued raising working cow horses. Corbin had always liked the cutting event, and had mentioned several times that he was interested in riding cutting horses. Dewitt and I knew Corbin had the ability to be an awesome cutter, and knew if he ever rode 'a shore nuf cuttin horse,' he would be hooked. God always has a plan, and this was no different. In January 2010, we wanted to buy a few head of cattle to add to our herd. We heard about a guy who had a small herd of about fifty head of mama cows that he needed to sell so Dewitt went to look at them. During the course of the conversation, they realized Dewitt's connection to Corbin, and it opened an entirely new subject. Dewitt told them Corbin was back competing in high school and open team ropings, but that he really wanted to cut. The problem was is that we didn't have a horse that we felt would be competitive. The gentleman said his dad had two finished cutting horses. He made the call to inquire as Dewitt was standing there, and just like that, Corbin had a horse. This was early January 2010.

The first rodeo back from the holiday break would be in late February, so Corbin had a lot of work to do getting the horse conditioned, and learning how to ride him to his advantage. Mr. Aymond, the horse owner, had a gelding and a mare, both sorrel, that he let Corbin and Colt bring to our house to get back into shape. The gelding was a little larger than the mare so the boys called them "Big'en" and "Little'en." Mr. Aymond told Corbin to ride them both, then make his choice of which one he liked best for competition. The boys rode them daily in an effort to quickly condition them for the upcoming cuttings. A friend of the family, Joe Higdon, had some buffalo that he had been working a few colts on, so Corbin hauled both horses to Joe's place several times each week to "tune them up." Eventually, at Mr. Aymond's suggestion, Corbin began hauling to Bo Boget's place a couple of times during the week so Bo could give Corbin some pointers on how to best show the horse.

The first rodeo of 2010 came, and was hosted by our own club, the Northeast Louisiana High School Rodeo Association. It was held at the Ike Hamilton facility in West Monroe, Louisiana. Corbin placed fourth in the cutting, and was off to a good start! Having won one of the shows, and placing in each of the others the rest of the season, Corbin ended the year after the state finals in fifth position. Only the top four finalists advance on to the national finals; however, one of the contestants knew immediately he would be unable to compete at the NHSFR which opened a spot for Corbin.

What an unbelievable journey we had been on for the past two years! In July 2008, Corbin was so severely injured that we were told he would never walk again and now, just two short years later, he was bound for competition at the NHSFR again! God is so good!

Heaven's Cowboy

Corbin riding "Big 'en" at the Northeast
Louisiana High Rodeo in West Monroe, Louisiana
in his first cutting show ever! He placed fourth.
February 2010
(photo courtesy: Watson's Photography)

Chapter 10

We spent Friday and Saturday of Easter weekend of 2010 in Salado, Texas for the Bloomer Team meeting. His third year of being a team member, as in 2009, Corbin again received the honor of being asked to serve as team captain. Each year, a professional photographer is on hand for photo shoots of each team member individually and as a group for Bloomer's advertising purposes. Justin Boot Company, along with Cinch and Cruel Girl, provide their latest product to be modeled by each team member during these photo sessions. Little did we know, the group was not only having still shots taken, but they were also being videoed. The videos made would be used for Bloomer Trailer commercials.

The highlight of the photo shoot was the night shoot that took place in a neighboring town to Salado which is Bartlett. The town was virtually abandoned that night, and gave the feeling of an old town one might see in the movies with it's brick streets, and old, weathered buildings. As we walked along the sidewalks, we noticed what appeared to be bullet holes in an abandoned bank building. One's mind wandered at the circumstances surrounding these bullet holes. If walls could talk…as the old saying goes.

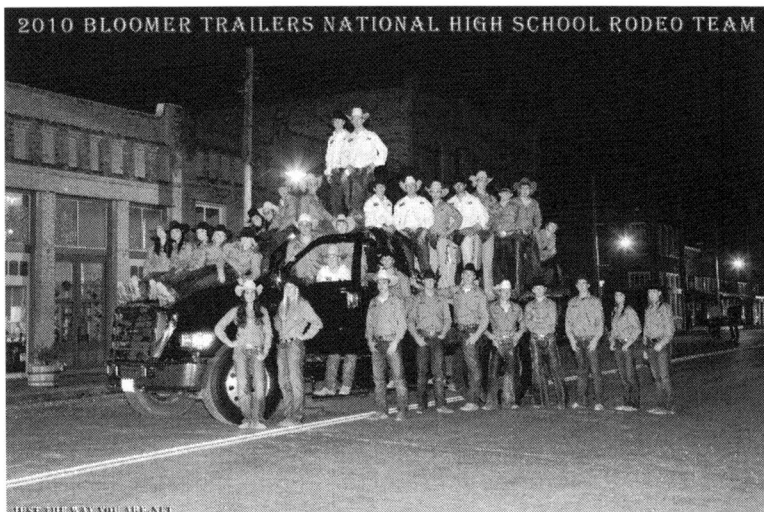

The 2010 Bloomer Trailers High School
Rodeo Team
Corbin is the tallest, wearing a light colored straw hat, standing on top of the truck

(Photo courtesy of Kathy Howerton/Just the Way You Are)

Being a huge John Wayne western movie fan, it was of particular interest when Kim Bloomer told me the new version of the movie *True Grit* was being filmed in Granger, the next town over. I wish we had had time to go there to watch some of the filming before we left the area. However, we were determined to get home in time to attend our church on Easter Sunday with the rest of our family. The Bloomers invited us to stay Saturday night to attend Easter church service with them, and although the offer was tempting, we decided to head for home. With that, we left Salado Saturday night following the annual barbeque for the Bloomer team members and their families. Corbin took the first driving shift. He set the inexpensive navigational system we had, and we were on our way back to Louisiana. It didn't take long for Colt and I to go completely out in the backseat of the truck, and soon Dewitt followed. I woke up around midnight, just in time to see a sign that said 'Houston.' Corbin had followed the directions the system gave but it had sent us too far south. We had traveled two hours out of the way making our trip four hours longer than necessary. I think we got home somewhere around 4:00 a.m.

∽

As the second half of the high school rodeo season was in full swing, it was disrupted when on April 20, 2010, Dewitt and I were awakened by a 4:00 a.m. phone call from our daughter, Courtney. She had just received a call from Transocean, the offshore drilling company Wyatt had been employed with for the past four plus years. From what Courtney gathered, there had been an apparent evacuation of Wyatt's rig, the Deepwater Horizon. No other information was given to her. This vague piece of information was all we had for what seemed endless hours.

Courtney and Wyatt had built a new home which they moved into the weekend following Corbin's arrival home from Baylor. It is located only four miles from our house, and was built on the corner of one of our pastures that is part of Silverside Plantation. I quickly dressed, and went to be with Courtney as she awaited further word. Grueling hours passed as we waited to hear from Transocean again, and more importantly, as we prayed to hear from Wyatt. Despite the many phone calls we made throughout the day trying to get news, we heard nothing.

Without going into detail as to all that happened in those long hours following the initial phone call we received, it wasn't until that afternoon we received confirmation that Wyatt was among the eleven missing crew members of the Deepwater Horizon. Still holding onto hope that the eleven men would be found, several heart wrenching days went by before we were able to talk to one of Wyatt's fellow crew members who told us he knew where Wyatt was working when the explosion happened. Despite Transocean's insistence that rescue teams continued searching, it became evident after talking to Wyatt's co-worker, Wyatt would not be coming home.

As one could imagine, Wyatt's death hit our entire family very hard. He had been very instrumental in Corbin's recovery, and they grew closer with each passing day. Months passed following Corbin's 2008 injury before he told us that while he was in ICU when Wyatt and Courtney were still in Farmington, he asked Wyatt what the doctors were saying regarding his condition. He also asked Wyatt if he would ever walk again. He knew Wyatt would tell him the truth, and not try to 'sugar coat' the situation. Wyatt told Corbin that he didn't know if he would or not, but he surely wouldn't if he didn't try, and work hard at it.

Wyatt had been a part of our lives for twelve years as he and Courtney had dated since they were sophomores in high school. Following Courtney's college graduation, they married, and spent five wonderful years together as husband and wife. As memories are renewed, I can't help remembering the weekend of their wedding. Courtney chose to have the wedding in the huge, secluded yard of my cousin's home near Manifest, Louisiana, which is only about ten miles north of where we live. It was a fairy tale wedding with the autumn leaves gently falling, and the rhythmic sound of the horse's hooves as the horse-drawn carriage brought her and Dewitt to the walk way that would lead her to Wyatt for the ceremony. The date of the wedding was October 30, and the boys had a rodeo that day in Jena. Because of taking wedding pictures, etc., they had to leave the rodeo without competing in all of their events. Corbin was sitting in first place to win the Champion All Around Cowboy saddle and title, and this being the last rodeo of the season meant he needed to compete in all of his events to hold on to that title. Sure enough, the young man who had been sitting second had a good rodeo, moved ahead of Corbin by a few points, and won. It became a family joke in the years to come that Courtney and Wyatt cost Corbin a saddle. I guess one could say we swapped a saddle for a son-in-law! It turned out to be an awesome swap, but I, for one, never let them forget it!

Wyatt was not only a hunting partner and friend to our sons, but had become more like a brother to them, and like a son to Dewitt and me. He was a fine Christian man who loved his Lord and Savior, and his family dearly. Dewitt and I are still proud to call him our son-in-law. Wyatt was twenty-seven -years-old and left behind his wife (our daughter) Courtney, and two precious, young daughters; Kaylee, who had just turned three-years-old only three days before the explosion, and Maddison, who was only three-months-old. Each of our hearts remains deeply saddened.

Colt, Corbin and Wyatt in a 2009 photo

Losing Wyatt affected Corbin in many ways, his roping included. The next few weeks mirrored the fact. Despite dealing with our tremendous sorrow, and trying to find a new normalcy after our loss, the next few months passed quickly, and we soon found ourselves headed back to Shawnee,

Oklahoma. Because Corbin was a high school senior, this would be the last time he would be eligible to compete in the IFYR rodeo. This time, Dewitt dropped everything he was doing, and came with us. Corbin, although still unable to compete in bull riding, was entered in team roping with header, Hayden Willson, his buddy from Monterey, Louisiana. Hayden had been Corbin's team roping partner during the 2007-2008 high school rodeo season prior to his injury. What a wonderful week it was and again, the Bloomer team won the rodeo, and was deemed the 2010 IFYR champion team!

We left Shawnee caravanning with four trailers of Louisiana cowboys and cowgirls. The trip was long but we managed to sight see along the way toward Gillette, Wyoming, where the 2010 NHSFR would be held. We visited the Crazy Horse monument and Mt. Rushmore. It is common knowledge that parking lots for most sight seeing attractions are not designed to accommodate large rigs. But don't let anyone tell you that a fifty-six foot truck and trailer rig can't get into the parking area designated for Mt. Rushmore! Though we received some strange looks from tourists as Dewitt made some fancy maneuvers making those tight corners, we did it! We found it well worth the detour and parking efforts as we enjoyed the awesome view, and cold ice cream on a hot day before we were off again toward the west.

༐

Corbin had qualified for the National Finals in Boys Cutting. Once we arrived and settled in, he and Josh Burns, another Louisiana cutter, practiced a couple of times prior to their first runs. Despite their practice efforts, neither did very well in the first round. Apparently, the horse Corbin was riding had some back pain, but for whatever reason, performed like he had never been in front of a cow before. Corbin was very disappointed to say the least. He practiced a few more times before his second cut, and this time did much better during the competition, scoring a 207. Neither Josh nor Corbin made the short round.

While in Gillette, Cinch had set up what is known at the NHSFR as Cinch Town. It was a huge room full of pool tables and electronic games for the kids to play during their "down time" while at the rodeo. In addition, each day, Susie Dobbs, co-host of RFD-TV's *Beyond Rodeo,* had daily interviews scheduled with some of the professional cowboys who had come by the NHSFR for a visit. In addition to some of the other Bloomer High School team members, Corbin was one of the cowboys Susie wanted to interview. Corbin was to be interviewed on Wednesday afternoon, and knowing this, I caught up with Susie late Tuesday to give her a copy of *Spurs, Chaps and Faith: The Corbin Carpenter Story,* the first book I authored about Corbin following his injury.

On Wednesday, Susie interviewed Corbin along with a couple of the other guys from the Bloomer Team. Unexpectedly, Susie asked me to come on stage to talk about the book, and a mother's perspective of the ordeal. Following our interview, Susie told us that when she read the book, she was so impressed with Pud that she wanted to meet this famous horse. I told her Pud was stalled on the fairgrounds so our interview went from Cinch Town to the hay field located behind the stall barns.

Pud was in prime form that bright and windy day, and Corbin and Susie had an awesome interview! They laughed and talked, and as I have said a hundred times before, it was "so Corbin" as his personality shined. Susie's daughter rode Pud for a few minutes, and we instantly became friends with both Susie and her friend, Brandon Rogers, who that day was serving as cameraman. The interview took place on July 22nd, Dewitt's birthday. He turned every shade of red as Susie, being a country music recording artist in addition to hosting *Beyond Rodeo*, sang her "Marilyn Monroe" version of *Happy Birthday* to him!

Following Corbin's accident in 2008, a rodeo family from Montana had sent Corbin gifts and had kept in contact with us via U. S. mail and email since that time. Since we both had children competing at the finals this year (2010), we had the privilege of finally meeting Skip and Holly Halmes and their family face to face. Though our families live many, many miles apart, and in a different part of the country, it was amazing all the similarities our families shared. We enjoyed a good meal, a great visit, and it was nice to meet them at last.

With several other Louisiana rodeo families in tow, on our way home from Gillette, we spent the night near Cheyenne, Wyoming. We had the privilege of attending the Saturday night performance of the Cheyenne Frontier Days Rodeos. Now competeing professionally, Louisiana cowboy Shane Hanchey was there, and Corbin enjoyed a visit with him. Shane and Tuff Cooper were hauling together at the time. Corbin knew Tuff from having competed with him almost each year beginning at the inaugural Wrangler Division (junior high) National Finals Rodeo seven years earlier. Corbin and Colt had dreamed of attending Cheyenne Frontier Days for a long while and both vowed to be competitors there someday!

Besides eating good food, visiting with great friends both old and new, and watching Corbin compete at the NHSFR again, perhaps some of the best things that came from the trip were not only Corbin's interview with Susie but also when he was awarded the WESA scholarship for $2,500 and another $500 scholarship. The 2010 National High School Finals Rodeo in Gillette, Wyoming, was a bittersweet end to Corbin's high school rodeo career. We had a great trip but still, neither Dewitt nor I could believe he had finished high school, and would soon be moving into another chapter of his life...college, and soon professional rodeo.

Heaven's Cowboy

Dewitt, Corbin and Theresa during senior
recognition night at the Northeast Louisiana High
School Rodeo, February 2010

(photo courtesy of Watson Photography)

Chapter 11

On Monday after we returned home from the national finals, Corbin, Colt and my nephew, Matt Evans, took the cutting horse Corbin had ridden back to his owner, Mr. Aymond, who lives south of Alexandria. A week or so before we left for the summer rodeos, a lady we knew whose daughter had high school rodeoed with Corbin, had given him a Toy Australian Shepherd puppy. She graciously agreed to keep the puppy until we returned home. Corbin's plan was to drop off "Big 'en," Mr. Aymond's horse, then meet our friend to pick up the puppy. The boys had successfully accomplished all they had set out to do. It had started drizzling rain as they were returning, and the roads were slick. They had already crossed the Red River Bridge between Alexandria and Pineville on their way home. As they crossed the next overpass, Corbin realized the right lane was closed with no signs forewarning them. Corbin quickly pulled the truck and twenty-eight foot horse trailer into the left lane but traffic had 'bottle necked' and was stopping. He applied his brakes, and his truck started skidding, not stopping until the front of it plowed into the rear of the18-wheeler that was ahead of him.

Corbin first called 9-1-1, and asked for a police officer to assist them, then called me. The words he said was so typical of him.

"Mom," he said, "You're not gonna be real happy about this, but...we've had a little fender bender."

"Is everybody okay?" I asked.

"Yes, mam, we're fine but the truck's not."

Corbin went on to give me the details of the accident, and said we were going to have to call a wrecker to take the truck to Cenla Body Shop, a business in Jonesville co-owned by John Manning, who is Lora White's brother.

As the conversation was nearing an end, I assured him his daddy would be on his way to get them. Again, I asked if he was sure everyone was alright.

Corbin said, "Oh, yes ma'am. My new little dog was sittin' beside me, and she didn't even fall off the seat."

As it turned out, the driver of the 18-wheeler told the police officer that he almost didn't get stopped either. The officer declared it was no one's fault because of the slick road conditions but mainly due to lack of signage before the overpass forewarning drivers of the lane closure. Corbin was not ticketed.

The cost of the damage to Corbin's truck was $6,000. It barely scratched the rear fender of the 18-wheeler. Trucks can be repaired or replaced. We were just so thankful no one was injured.

∽

The starting dates of college classes at Northwestern State University was fast approaching, and because we had been so busy rodeoing all summer, Corbin was not yet registered for the fall semester. Corbin's intention was to take internet courses, and as many classes as he could in our home town of Jonesville at the satellite school provided by Northwestern. However, as time approached, there was very little student interest in the Jonesville classes so the university completely did away with them for that semester. Likewise, classes in the neighboring town of Jena did not make, and were also cancelled. Because of this, none of the classes Corbin wanted and needed to take would be available locally. He did not want to move to Natchitoches if at all possible. Knowing this, Corbin and I drove to the main campus to schedule classes. He wanted to continue his business of breaking and training horses while in school so we were hopeful his schedule would be compatible.

After spending an hour or more in the office of a most helpful employee of Northwestern, we left Natchitoches with twelve hours of college classes scheduled. He would be taking three internet courses along with one night class, Biology: The Study of the Human Body, in Alexandria which is an hour drive from our home. Corbin and I spent a wonderful day together, and even managed to allow enough time to have lunch, while in Natchitoches, with our cousin, Rae Anne Firmin, who is employed with the local newspaper as editor of the society section.

∽

The first Wednesday of classes rolled around, and Corbin was off to Alexandria. We still find it humorous when we think of his first question and comments to us upon his arrival home that night. The first words he spoke were, "Mom, are you sure I'm in the right class?"

To which I replied, "That's what your advisor said you should take. Why?"

"Well, at the beginning of class, the professor asked how many of us were in nursing. I was the only person who DIDN'T raise his hand. Then he asked how many of us were seniors. I just sort of scratched my head kind of like I might be raising my hand 'cause I just didn't know WHAT was going on," Corbin explained.

That was typical of Corbin, and of course, we had to laugh. As Corbin talked on about his new class, he told us how 'cool' his professor was, and how excited he was about all he had learned in his first three hour timeframe of this "live class," as he called it.

Obviously, Corbin was an avid participant in class discussions. After a couple of weeks of his "live classes," he came home one night telling us that his fellow classmates must have thought everything he said was funny because each time he stood, and said something, everyone laughed. He also said he just didn't understand it because he felt sure he had the answers right. Knowing Corbin as we do, we understood.

My friend, Lora White, once made the statement, "Other than him getting hurt, there were very few serious moments with Corbin."

The humorous part of that statement is that most of the time he didn't even know he was being funny. We know all too well that typically it wasn't WHAT Corbin said but rather, HOW he said it or his facial expressions.

(L to R) Zack Wright, Colter White, Tell Burley and Corbin all posed for a picture prior to the LHSRA rodeo performance in Eunice, LA . Spring 2010

Theresa Freeman Carpenter

(L to R) Courtney, Maddison, Colt, Kaylee and Corbin. At the beach in Ft. Walton Beach, Florida for a friend's wedding. August 2010

Heaven's Cowboy

Corbin saying the opening prayer for the
2009 Northeast Louisiana High School Rodeo,
February 2009
(photo courtesy of Derrell's Photography)

An interview with Pam Minick at the 2009
Bloomer Trailer
Rodeo Team meeting. In the background, Clay
O'Brien Cooper
on left and Randy Bloomer on right.
(photo courtesy of Kathy Howerton/Just The Way
You Are)

Heaven's Cowboy

Riding with a friend. David Alvin Chevallier on the left, Corbin on the right. 2009

(photo courtesy of Liz Condo)

Photo taken before a winter 2009 duck hunt.
(L to R) Colt, Corbin and Lee

Wyatt, Ethan House and Corbin showing off the Rattlesnake they killed on our hunting property. 2007

Theresa Freeman Carpenter

Front row L to R: Colt, Lisha Bond, Erica Hammons, Jadie Hammons
Back row L to R: Shane Hood, Codie Poe, Corbin
May 2010

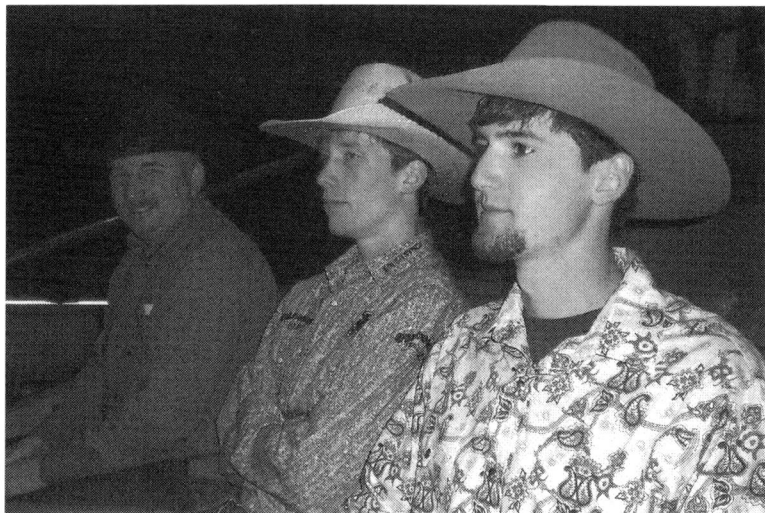

Dewitt, Corbin and Slade Deason settle in to watch one of the March 2009 performances of the Timed Event Championship in Guthrie, Oklahoma.
Corbin spoke during Cowboy Church that morning.

Corbin and Colt on the beach in Ft. Walton, Florida, August 2010

As I look at the pictures from this trip to the beach, I am reminded of the night before our friend's wedding when a group, including the bride and groom, Caylon (Deason) and Cody Mitchell, was sitting on the beach visiting. Cody, having been in the Marines, had several buddies of whom he served with in the military, present for the wedding. Corbin had never met these guys before. The conversation soon turned to Corbin breaking his neck. One of the guys in particular, seemed to never be at a loss for words. He kept insisting they were teasing, and that it couldn't be so. However, Slade Deason continued trying to convince the guy otherwise. During the entire conversation, Corbin didn't say a word. Somewhat convinced, finally, the young man asked Corbin how it happened. Not to allow him to get anything over him, Corbin calmly replied, "Stuff like that happens when you party naked."

The remark left the guy totally speechless which was Corbin's intention! I don't know to this day, if anyone ever told the Marine the true story.

Theresa Freeman Carpenter

A typical day for Corbin at the Bar CC; riding his favorite horse, Pud, checking cattle, and working his dogs. 2009

(photo courtesy of Liz Condo)

On September 22, 2010, Corbin was about five weeks into his first semester at college when returning home from his night class in Alexandria. He called me shortly after 9:00 p.m. on this particular Wednesday night saying he was going to meet one of his friends, and shine for coons across the road from our house. He said he would be home shortly. Dewitt, Colt and I went to bed about 10:00 and had just fallen to sleep when we were awakened by the ringing of the telephone. I answered, and it was a neighbor who lives about two miles down the road from us, saying there had been a bad accident, and Corbin was in it. I asked him if Corbin was okay, and all he would tell me is that it was pretty bad. I immediately began praying as I woke up Dewitt and Colt. We were snatching on clothes as quickly as possible. Although the Louisiana weather was still warm, I remember looking into my closet, and grabbing a warm up suit that had a jacket, thinking it may be cold in the hospital if Corbin had to go.

As we drove up to the sight of the accident, blue lights were flashing, and I could see only the driver's side of the truck belonging to the friend who had been driving. The passenger side had come to a rest against a large tree. Both Dewitt and I jumped out, and started toward the truck. I remember my distant cousin, Carol Prudhomme, looking at me with tears in her eyes, saying "Theresa, don't go."

I remember falling on my knees to the ground, crying. I'm not sure exactly where

Dewitt was but eventually he made his way to the truck. Later he told me that he approached on the driver's side, and Corbin's friend, although badly injured, was coherent, saying "Mr. Dewitt, I'm so sorry." Dewitt saw Corbin but he and I have never discussed it.

I don't know how long I was on the ground but somehow, I convinced myself that Corbin was trapped in the truck, and was going to be all right. My thoughts went back to the time when Lee was about fifteen-years-old, and was in an auto accident. It was raining, and he was riding with his cousin. They started to pass an eighteen-wheeler, only to realize the truck was making a left hand turn. Lee's cousin whipped the truck back in, hitting the eighteen wheeler in the rear. The main blow to the truck was on the passenger side where Lee was riding. He was trapped but was soon freed, and taken to the hospital. There he received stitches over his right eye, in his right upper lip, and had to have some dental work. Although he was several weeks recovering, his injuries were not life threatening. I prayed it would be the same for Corbin.

I also remember thinking that God had picked up my son out of the dirt in that arena just over two years before, and brought him from being paralyzed to riding cutting horses. I was convinced that God would do it again, regardless of what anyone told me. I immediately stopped crying, and got back into my truck. Colt was in the back seat crying his heart out. I told him not to cry, Corbin would be all right. I remember telling everyone who came to me that Corbin would be okay, they just had to get him out of the truck. I remember asking what hospital they would take him to, but no one answered.

Finally, I saw Dewitt walking toward me. A man had him by the arm, helping him walk as he was crying uncontrollably. As he approached me, I told him to stop crying, Corbin would be okay. He looked me in the eyes with tears streaming down his face, and said, "Tree" (a nickname my brother gave me as a child), and shook his head from side to side.

I cried out, "Don't tell me that, just don't tell me that." It was then I knew God had taken my sweet baby home.

Colt remained in the back seat of my truck with Carol. He was heart broken as were we all. He and Corbin spent everyday together when Colt wasn't in school. They hunted, rode horses, fed cattle, and worked in the hay field. Everything they did was together. Later, during the days immediately following, I was told two things that will forever stay with me regarding Corbin and Colt. First of all, Carol sat in the backseat with Colt at the wreck site. She told me that as he cried to her, he told her that he didn't know what he would do without his big brother. Also, my friend, Cynthia Brown, told me that Corbin had come to her shop to get his hair cut one day while Colt was at school. There were five or six other guys there at the same time. Cynthia said, as Corbin quietly sat and listened, he absorbed the words of each of the boys as they took turns telling why they didn't want their little brothers or sisters trailing along with them. When they were done, Cynthia told me that without hesitation, Corbin said, "Well you boys may not want your little brothers or sisters with you, but I love my little brother, and I want him with me all the time." According to Cynthia, the conversation ended with that.

⁓

By the time I knew the reality of the situation, among many other people, my brother and sister-in-law, Chris and Stacy Freeman, had arrived at the wreck site. Chris had been calling to inform other family members and close friends. Dewitt insisted Chris take Colt and me to Courtney's house to break the terrible news to her. We were unsure how she would handle such horrible news, after all, not only were she and Corbin very close, but she, like the rest of us, was still dealing with losing her husband only five months and two days before. Word was traveling quickly in our small community, and we thought it important to tell Courtney before she received a phone call from someone asking her about the accident. Besides telling Courtney that Wyatt wouldn't be coming home, telling her about her little brother was one of the hardest things we've ever faced. Thank God my brother was there to actually say the words.

Within the hour of reaching Courtney's house, friends and family members began gathering. My brother left to tell my parents, who I knew would take it hard. By daylight, including my parents, our siblings and numerous friends, there were countless people at Courtney's house. It was dejavu from just five months before as word spread about Wyatt. My mind drifted to the conversation Dewitt and I had earlier in the year following Maddison's birth in January. We were so proud at how our little family had grown in such a short period of time. In five years, two of our children had married, and given us three precious grandchildren with another on the way. Now, it seemed that God was taking them away just as quickly. Our hearts are broken.

Not sure of how the accident happened, the young man later told us he had been drinking prior to Corbin getting into the truck with him. He said a dog or some type animal ran out in front of the truck. The driver swerved in an attempt to miss it, lost control, went off the road, and crashed into the tree, hitting on the passenger's side where Corbin was sitting. Our son was killed instantly.

Corbin met this young man at a summer church camp a couple of years earlier. He told us he knew his friend was going down the wrong path, and was looking for something. Corbin knew he needed the Lord, and was trying to be an example to him.

Chapter 14

Like any parent, it was always our prayer we would never have to bury our children. I can remember when a similar tragedy happened to someone else, I couldn't imagine what the parents were going through, and hoped and prayed we never would. Having lost Wyatt, and now Corbin, we know all too well the feeling of deep sorrow, and the never ending, wrenching pain of a broken heart. Even so, God was giving us strength to deal with a task that we had prayed would never come to pass, as we planned the funeral of one of our precious children.

I remembered seeing western/cowboy design coffins in some of the western magazines, and several people immediately went to work looking through each magazine we had on hand, trying to find the name of some of the companies. I don't remember who found it on the internet, but a call was made, and an appropriate one was located near Lake Charles. Our friends, Linda and Mike McCartney, without any reservation, took off to south Louisiana to get it, then delivered the coffin to the funeral home. They made the trip before I ever realized they were gone. The coffin was made of knotty pine, and was built in the 'old timey' fashion like you see in the western movies. The lid opened from one end to the other, and it was shaped similar to a person's body. It had leather handles. Dewitt, Lee, Bill Brown, and Billy Carlton took our branding iron to the funeral home, and burned the Bar CC brand on all four sides. So I heard later, they became somewhat panic stricken when Dewitt first touched the hot iron to the wood as it flamed up. I assume it was the finish on the wood that was flammable. No harm was done, and if one had not heard the story, there was no evidence of it on the coffin. I'm sure Corbin was laughing from above as each man bolted to put out the small flame. No other coffin would have suited Corbin's personality any better. He would have loved it.

The wake was scheduled for Friday night, September 24, 2010 at our church, Pleasant Grove Baptist, just north of our hometown. The funeral would be the next morning at

11:00 a.m. Dewitt called Tilt James, the gentleman we had come to know so well following Corbin's 2008 injury. We were so blessed that each of us, including Corbin, saw Tilt, and was able to visit with him during the National Finals High School Rodeo in July, just two months before. Tilt would now be flying in from New Mexico to take part in Corbin's funeral service.

Our pastor, Reverend Craig James, would also preach part of the service. Brother Craig had only been at our church for about six or seven months, yet we had grown to love him and his family in that short time. We felt as though we had known them for a lifetime. I will never forget the first time Brother Craig met Corbin. It was his first day as Pastor of our church. When service was dismissed that morning, he went to the front door to personally meet and greet everyone as they left the building. He asked each person who they were, and when Corbin said his name, the look on our pastor's face showed his surprise. Brother Craig told Corbin he had been praying for him for two years, and had no idea he would now be his pastor!

Sadly, he now found himself preaching his funeral. He had already taken part in Wyatt's memorial service only a few months before. The first time he and Wyatt met was when Maddison had to be hospitalized for acid reflux when she was only a month or so old. Unannounced, Brother Craig walked into Maddison's hospital room, and saw Wyatt reading the Bible to Courtney. They visited for a while, and had an instant connection. I'll never forget Brother Craig telling the congregation that story during Wyatt's service. Now, in just a few months of knowing him, Brother Craig preached the funerals of two of our close family members. We are so blessed to have this man of God as our pastor, especially during the trying times we were facing.

Dewitt and I also asked Randy Bloomer to take part in the service. Although we had only known the Bloomer family for the past three or four years, we had become good friends with him and his family. Not only that, Corbin admired and respected Randy and Kim very much. During the service, Randy brought humor to an otherwise somber crowd as he gave an awesome example of how Corbin always wanted people to feel good about themselves. He said Corbin had just arrived at the fairgrounds in Shawnee when they were walking together across the parking lot back to the trailers. Corbin was wrestling around and playing with Randy as he often did. Randy was feeling really down on himself, and said something like, "Corbin, I'm just getting too old.

Corbin looked at Randy, smiled and said, "Well, Mr. Randy, I'm not saying you're gettin' any older, but I'm pretty sure you're not gettin' any younger."

Randy then said, "My gosh, you're going to be a politician."

To which Corbin replied, "I don't think so. I'm too honest for that."

Like many, Randy, Kim, Alexis and Jake were heart broken to hear the tragic news of Corbin's passing. Randy said that Corbin was one of the people closest to him that he had ever lost. Corbin would have felt the same way had the table been turned.

Several years ago when Jesse McClure helped with our cattle, he and Corbin spent endless hours together. Though Jesse was about five and a half years older than Corbin, they became the best of friends. After Jesse graduated from high school, he moved to Texas to work on a large ranch. I vividly remember his first visit back home. Although I knew Jesse was coming to visit, Corbin did not. In my mind, I can still see Jesse standing on the carport when Corbin opened the door, realized it was him, and dove off of the top step into Jesse's arms. Corbin learned some of his horsemanship skills from Jesse through the many hours they spent checking cattle and breaking colts. Their adventures on the ranch became the subject matter of several poems I have written. It was during the time when Jesse was working that my dad gave me a series of Red Steagall cassettes that we listened to for hours on end. A particular song that Corbin loved was *One Empty Cot in the Bunkhouse* which tells about a cowboy who had passed away, leaving an empty cot, and a string of horses that was never ridden again. Corbin said then, "When me and Jesse die, y'all will have to play that song at our funerals."

At the time, I had no idea, we would actually find ourselves doing so. How appropriate the words were for Corbin. During the service, when Red Steagall sang the part about mending fences, I couldn't help but look at Dewitt and smile, knowing that was one of Corbin's least liked chores.

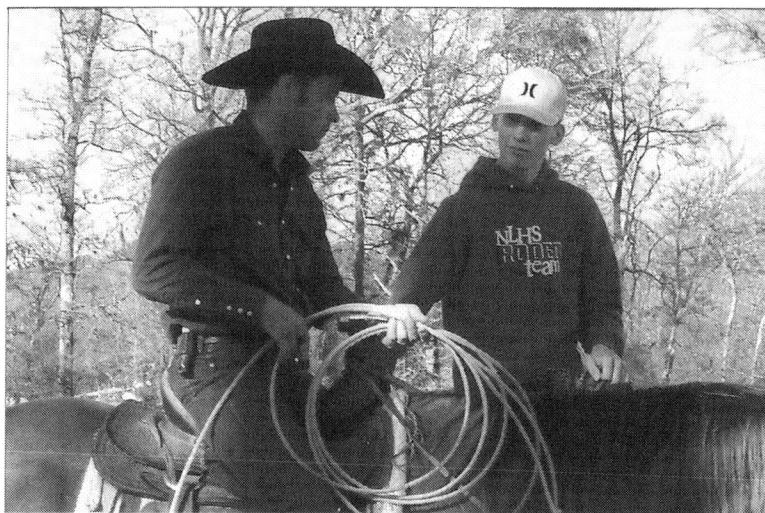

Jesse McClure and Corbin exchanging stories as they roped at our house. Corbin is wearing his favorite "hoodie." Spring 2009

Susie Dobbs, who is co-host of *Beyond Rodeo* on RFD-TV, had interviewed Corbin earlier in the summer. When Corbin passed away, Susie was performing at a state fair in one of the northern states but nonetheless, was trying to make arrangements to fly in to sing at Corbin's service. Due to circumstances beyond her control, she was unable to do so. However, her friend, Brandon Rogers, who graciously served as her camera man during the NHSFR rodeo in Gillette, attended. He brought with him a DVD that Susie had recorded for the service. She included an excerpt of the interview filmed in July, some pictures of Corbin, and a song, *Rodeo Road*. The interview was very uplifting, and as I have said many times, was "so Corbin." His vivacious personality gleamed throughout their visit, and we are so blessed to have this footage. Susie's song was awesome and very appropriate for Corbin. Though she couldn't be there physically, we knew her heart was present.

A shot taken during Corbin's interview with Susie Dobbs at the NHSFR in Gillette, Wyoming, July 2010

One other song was played during the service, *In the Garden* by Brad Paisley. It was supposed to have been the version sung by my cousin, Gerald Huffman, but somehow, the CD's got swapped. Either way, it was beautiful, and was the same version played at Wyatt's memorial service.

With Corbin having so many close friends, it was a very difficult task to name only a few as pallbearers. However, serving in that capacity were Colter White, Slade Deason, Ethan House, David Austin Chevallier, Shane Hood, Corey Granger, Chris Shivers, Mike White, Jake Hebert, Hayden Willson, Jesse McClure, Lee White, and Colten Blanchard. Honorary pallbearers were members of the Louisiana High School Rodeo Association, the Bloomer Trailer Rodeo Team Members, and a host of friends.

At the cemetery, Lenora and Dan Daily drove their horse and wagon carrying the western style coffin to Corbin's final resting place in the Carpenter plot at Heard Cemetery in Manifest. Bill Brown held Pud as the wagon passed. Bill said Pud lowered her head as they passed with the coffin. It is our belief that she knew it was Corbin. Bill handed Pud's reins to Slade Deason, who then led her behind the wagon as the pallbearers followed. Our family, and the hundreds of friends who attended the graveside service, walked behind to the grave site.

During the service at the cemetery, our long time friend, Reverand Jimmy Keene, spoke. Before the service started, Brother Craig leaned down to me and said "Did you hear that?" I had. In the distance, Pud whinnied as if she were telling her best friend good bye.

Going to Corbin's final resting place.
September 25, 2010
(photo courtesy of David Ryan)

Theresa Freeman Carpenter

Countless people came to the cemetery
for the burial.
Notice Pud in the center of the picture.
(photo courtesy of David Ryan)

When Dewitt asked Slade to lead Pud,
Slade started crying uncontrollably. It was
some weeks later until we were told that
prior to Corbin's death, he had told Slade
he wanted him to lead Pud to his graveside
when he died. We had no idea when we
asked Slade, that Corbin had already
asked him to do so.

It has been said that Corbin wrote his own funeral, so to speak. I believe this is so as evidenced by the number of people who were present for his wake, funeral, and graveside services. We were told that approximately 3,000 people attended the wake on Friday night. Since then, numerous people have told me they came by our church, and because of their health or for whatever reason, couldn't stand in the long line to get into the church. Several people told me they had to park their vehicles well over a mile from the church parking lot. We were told there was another 1,000 plus people attending the funeral, most of which had to stand outside due to lack of seating inside our church building.

Among the large number of people who attended, Tuff Hedeman left a CBR bull riding early to fly into Jonesville to attend. Flying in with him was Chandler Bownds, a former Bloomer Team member from west Texas, now riding CBR. Kelsey Drilling from Cinch Clothing came in with the Bloomer family as did countless other people. I heard people whispering about the long truck and trailer rigs that were parked near our church. These belonged to cowboys and cowgirls who had made a detour to Jonesville on their way to a rodeo somewhere, just to pay their respects. We remain very humbled that each and everyone made such an effort to give their condolences, and pay their respects to our family and this giant of a cowboy.

❧

Paul Daily and his family, wife Joanna, and children, Lenora and Dan, travel across the United States giving testimony, comparing our lives to that of a wild horse. Paul explains how, like a wild horse, we run around in circles with no where to go until we trust God, and become submissive to His will. In approximately two hours, Paul and his children can have an unbroken horse saddled, and riding, sometimes even lying on the ground at their command. The day of the funeral, September 25, 2010, they were giving such a demonstration in Kentucky. Paul later told us that during the exact time Corbin's funeral was in progress, God lead him to tell the people at the demonstration about our son. He took the little *Way for Cowboys Bible* that contained Corbin's testimony, and walked through the crowd showing them Corbin's picture. He told them of his injury, and how God brought him through it to compete in rodeo again. He told them of the auto accident that took Corbin's life only four days before, and as the demonstration was going on, he was being buried. He explained that death could come to any of us anytime, and how each of us needs to be living for the Lord, have our lives in order, and be ready to go to our heavenly home at any given time. According to the Daily family, eleven people came to know the Lord that day. The following day brought another wild horse demonstration in another location and again, eleven more people were lead to Christ. Praise God! Corbin's testimony lives on.

Chapter 15

Even during sad times, there is always humor if one would take time to recognize it. Dewitt was in the middle of a dirt job on Louisiana Delta, a huge area of basically farmland south of Jonesville. Being on a tight schedule to finish the project, he returned to work the Monday following Corbin's funeral. The job consisted of installing several drainage structures, and to do so, he and the crew cleaned out the large ditches that would house the structures. The project was nearing completion; therefore, the grass and weeds had been removed from the area leaving only exposed dirt. In fact, at this particular location, the culverts had already been installed, and finishing touches were being done. Dewitt recalls standing alone in the open field near the structure when he bent down to pickup something. He said he felt a gust of wind, similar to a whirlwind, try to take his hat from his head. He reached to the top of his straw cowboy hat quickly, and pushed it as far down on his head as possible. In just an instant, it happened again, this time claiming his hat. He watched as it flew across the open levee but by the time he laid down what he was holding, and crossed the levee, the straw hat was no where in site. Dewitt searched the entire area including inside the structure. He searched again the next day without success. The hat was gone and to this day has not been located.

Dewitt called telling me what had happened. Being the prankster that Corbin was, there was no doubt it was him who was playing a trick on his dad. I could picture Corbin laughing with one hand over his mouth, and pointing at his dad with the other. Courtney declared we got just what we deserved, sending a cowboy away without a hat. Lee simply said, "That's Corbin."

∽

I've always heard that we can't control our dreams, and perhaps this is so. It is my belief that dreams are sometimes God's way of comforting us or revealing something to us. We read about God's revelations to people throughout the Bible.

With that said, I feel this book would not be complete without the inclusion of a few of the dreams experienced by our family members and friends.

Only a few weeks following Corbin's funeral, I heard Colt crying as I walked into his room to wake him for school one morning. Through his sobbing, he told me he had dreamed about Corbin. He said Corbin was standing across the gate near our barn, smiling. He told Colt, "I'm all right, buddy. I'd better be gettin' back up there. I'm sorry, but I have to go now."

Colt was crying out, "No, no, no, don't leave me."

A couple of nights later, Dewitt dreamed Corbin was standing at what he described was almost the same place as in Colt's dream. Witt said as he approached, Corbin was grinning from ear to ear, and extended his hand to shake. Dewitt asked him what he had been doing. Corbin told him that he was doing what he loved, going down the road, ridin' bulls.

A couple of months had passed when one of my dearest friends, Lora White, shared with me her daughter's dream. Lora and Darrell's children, Colter and Jessi, have spent many hours with our boys both rodeoing, and simply hanging out. Jessi, is the same age as Colt and Colter is two years younger than Corbin. The White's, as well as Lora's parent's, Conley and Sue Manning, are like family to us, and rightfully so as Darrell is my cousin. Our families have shared hundreds of meals together, more laughs than I can remember, many practice runs either at our arena or theirs, and lots of rodeos that brought us home during the wee hours of the morning.

One morning as Lora White was waking her daughter, Jessi, for school, she told her mom that she had dreamed we were having a huge party for Corbin. He had been at a rodeo where bull riding and calf roping were the only events. In her dream, Corbin had won both, and we were giving a party in his honor. Immediately, it came to Lora that those were the two events Corbin had enjoyed with success prior to his injury. She told Jessi that now Corbin was in heaven, he was again winning in the two events he had been unable to compete in since 2008.

∽

Obie Jefferson is a fine Christian who has kept our children since before Courtney was born. She has watched each of them grow and prosper, and is now doing the same with our grandchildren. Obie has shared in our family's happy times and sad times. She helped Dewitt's parents during the time my father-in-law was ill and passed away in 2003 as a result of Parkinsons Disease. Obie is a jewel, and it would have been very difficult for me to work all of these years without her help. We are so blessed she is part of our lives. Having lost a son herself, Obie knows all too well what we are going through. It is because she is close to our children that she shares in the sorrow of our loss. I believe this is the reason she, too, saw Corbin in a dream. In Obie's dream, she saw Corbin standing in the hallway of our home with that big smile spread across his face. He simply told her that he was all right.

As of this writing, Corbin has yet to come to me in a dream. Some say I am not ready, and perhaps they are right. I envy those who have seen him and talked with him again.

⌒⌒

As stated many times, Corbin had a unique way with animals which was proven by his bond with Pud. After he died, each of us was concerned about Pud's wellbeing, not because she wasn't cared for, but because of the close bond she and Corbin shared. I feel in my heart that she knew Corbin was gone as evidenced by her actions at the cemetery. In the days that followed, we were worried that Pud would stop eating but thankfully, she did not. Lora mentioned that perhaps his lengthy stay when he was injured prepared her for his absence.

Like Pud, Corbin shared a bond with his dogs. Corbin especially liked yellow, black mouthed Cur dogs for working cattle and hog hunting. He and Chris Shivers traded back and forth until Corbin ended up with a male named Yeller, and a female he called Belle. Corbin could do anything with them simply by talking to them. He took them each time we worked cattle, and far more times than not, they earned their keep.

Early in the summer 2010 on one of Corbin and Chris' trips to south Louisiana working cattle, Jacob Greer gave Corbin a pretty little, yellow, black mouthed Cur puppy that he named Little Susie. He worked her around the house baying calves some but because she was still young, he hadn't taken her to the big pastures yet. Little Susie loved Corbin and missed him terribly. Two days after we lost Corbin, Little Susie stopped eating. At six months old, and only ten days after Corbin passed away, Little Susie died. She literally grieved herself to death.

∽

After Corbin's injury, John Bache built a pair of roping spurs for Corbin. They had a short shank on them, just as Corbin liked. These first spurs were sort of an experimental job for John, and later he built a custom pair very similar, but with Corbin's name and Bar CC brand on them. Slade Deason loved both pair, and tried to talk Corbin into giving him his old ones. It was too late, however, he had already given them to Colt. Corbin talked to John about building Slade a pair that he would give to him as a Christmas gift.

Christmas 2010 was a very difficult time for us with two of our family members missing. However, we knew Corbin was present with us when John's son, Lance, delivered to us not only the pair of roping spurs he made for Slade, but little did we know, Corbin had ordered a custom pair for Colt as well. It made us very happy to surprise these boys with such a special gift but at the same time, it was very, very emotional for all of us.

∽

Ethan House, Zack Wright, and Colter White have been lifelong friends with my boys, and have spent hours on end at our house. Like several other of our boy's friends, we feel like they are part of our family. Colt,

Corbin, Ethan, Zack, and Colter White wrestled and played constantly. In fact, I still have a perfectly round hole the size of a baseball near the floor on the back wall of my hall where "someone's heel" went through. I have thought about repairing it many times, but it serves as a reminder of the laughter and good times they had that day, not long before Corbin passed away. During the many times they would wrestle, the older boys took advantage of Colt because of his size. I kept telling them that one of these days, Colt was going to grow up and "knock the fire" out of them for all the tricks they had pulled on the little fellow. Being the good sport that Colt is, he wrestled right along with them, and gave it his best shot. Now, at thirteen-years-old, Colt is making a big guy, and they sure wouldn't get away with those tricks now!

It was mid March 2011, almost six months after Corbin died. Our pastor, Bro. Craig James, was visiting. Dewitt, Brother Craig, and I were standing outside just off of our carport while Colt was sitting on the tailgate of my truck. Dewitt had told Brother Craig about the hat ordeal that happened on the jobsite right after the funeral. Then, Colt began telling about how after Corbin was injured and returned home, he told Corbin that while he was still in a wheelchair, he might be able to get a lick or two in on him. It was about the time Colt was laughing, telling us that Corbin could still take him, wheelchair and all, that a bird flew over, and pooped on the collar of Colt's shirt. We all laughed even more. Brother Craig said, "That was big brother telling you he can still get the best of you!" That Corbin is still playing tricks.

Because of the great respect people had for Corbin, the inspiration he was to so many, and the legacy he left behind, many tributes have been paid to him including a scholarship program, a memorial buckle program, a national communications line, and a number of others. Many of these programs have and will be beneficial to students not only in Louisiana but people nationwide.

When Corbin passed away, our family set up a scholarship fund right away at a local bank in his memory. Many memorial contributions have been made to this important program. As parents, we appreciate the scholarships Corbin had been awarded during his high school rodeo career. These scholarships would have allowed him to attend college for at least two years, with no out of pocket expenses for tuition and books. When he placed ninth at the NHSFR in 2007, he was awarded a PBR (Professional Bull Riding) scholarship and one from Corral West. In 2008 following his injury, he was awarded the "Tough Luck" award which is given each year to a cowboy and cowgirl who competed at the NHSFR without success, usually due to an injury sustained while competing there. As a senior, Corbin was awarded the WESA scholarship (Western and English Sales Association). He was also chosen to receive a local scholarship from our rural electric company, Concordia Electric. With the contributions received, the Corbin Carpenter Memorial Scholarship will be awarded annually to a deserving cowboy or cowgirl during the Louisiana High School Rodeo state finals.

∽

After Corbin's injury, we gave our testimony at Hineston Tabernacle in Hineston, Louisiana. We were asked by a rodeo family we had become very close to during our travels, Max and Stacy Bonnette. The day we spent with these awesome people of God, afforded us many friendships including that of Roger and Sissy Carroll. Since then, these people have become like family to us, and now serve a role in our lives far more than we could have ever imagined. Roger and Sissy have relatives who rodeoed on the junior high and high school level and they attended most of the rodeos. During the early part of 2010, Roger came to Dewitt at a high school rodeo and told him he had a horse he wanted to give our son. Dewitt said that although we appreciate the gesture, Corbin really didn't need anymore horses because we had so many.

Roger said, "First of all, it's not for Corbin. God told me to give this horse to Colt."

With that, Dewitt gladly accepted the young filly. He said, "If God told you to give that horse to Colt, then we had better take it because you just don't argue with God!"

In the weeks to come, Roger brought the little mare to us, and Corbin and Colt began working with her. This horse became very special to Colt, not only because she was going to be trained to cut cattle, but she would prove to be one of the last horses Corbin would start.

Following the 2010 state junior high finals, Roger realized a need for additional awards to be given to the winners and finalists. Shortly after Corbin died, Roger called saying the awards program should be in memory of Corbin. With that, the Corbin Carpenter Memorial Buckle Program was born. In just four short months, our committee managed to raise almost $11,000 through private and corporate contributions that enables us to award 104 trophy belt buckles to the Champion and Reserve Champion average winners, and the Champion and Reserve Champion go-around winners at the junior high state finals. We will continue raising money, because, like the scholarship program, this awards program will be an annual project.

∽

During the days that followed Corbin's funeral, I received several phone calls from Siri Stevens, owner and editor of *The Rodeo News* magazine. Siri, a fine Christian lady, had been faithful to follow Corbin's 2008 injury and recovery. She never passed an opportunity to interview him when they showed up at the same rodeos. Siri wrote a feature story about Corbin that appeared in the May 1, 2009 issue, with a picture of Corbin coming over the head of the bull, M33, gracing the front cover. Now, Siri was very supportive of our tremendous loss, one she stated was felt by the entire rodeo world. Siri told me about a young cowboy who had been killed in an auto accident nearly a year before, and asked if his mother could call me. Of course, I said yes. A few days later, his mom called, and the two of us shared our similar stories. As I sat in Corbin's room, in the silence, looking at his belongings, I found it to be a great comfort to talk to another mom who had gone through a similar tragedy.

A couple of months passed when Siri called again saying that God had laid something upon her heart, and she wanted to share it with me. She said that in her business, it is not uncommon for her to hear about fallen cowboys and cowgirls shortly after the tragedies take place. She felt God leading her to suggest a "nationwide communications line" open to families of anyone who had suffered a loss or a life changing injury. She went on to say that because I had experienced both, she felt that God was telling her I was the one to do this. After much prayer, I accepted the challenge. It is my prayer that through our experiences, God will allow my family to help others. Perhaps this program was all part of God's plan when He took Corbin home.

∽

In late fall 2010, royal blue rubber commemorative bracelets were being sold in Corbin's memory. As far as I know, it was Molly Milner from south Louisiana who started this. The royal blue bracelets made in Corbin's memory say "Ridin' for heaven's cowboy – forever in our hearts CC." I have been wearing mine constantly since it was given to me during our first rodeo of the 2010-2011 season. If memory serves me correctly, I was told there have been well over 1,000 sold with proceeds going to the Justin Crisis Fund in Corbin's memory.

∾

On one of my almost daily trips to the post office to pick up our morning mail, I received a package from an unknown address. Much to my surprise, when I opened it, it was a gorgeous turquoise necklace with Corbin's picture on the front of the pendant, and the poem I wrote in 2006 entitled, *Corbin's Prayer,* on the reverse side. I cried uncontrollably. Even not knowing who it was from, I was very thankful to have it. A couple of weeks later, a phone call from Lauren Landry of Kuttinupjewelry confirmed not only the person who gave it to me, but it's designer. Since that time, Lauren has a full line of 'one of a kind' Corbin jewelry available via internet. Thank you very much, Lauren, for a piece of jewelry I will forever cherish and wear humbly.

∾

One of the magazine articles about Corbin following his death appeared in the October 15, 2010 issue of *Rodeo News* and was written by Kallan Mudd, a Louisiana cowgirl who was elected to serve as NHSRA secretary in 2008. Kallan also wrote a poem that appeared with the article. She is a beautiful and talented young lady who writes an awesome bi-monthly feature article for the magazine called *"Kallan's Corner."* I look forward to reading it in each issue. After reading this particular article, I asked Kallan if she would mind if I printed excerpts that was written to honor Corbin. Kallan wrote:

> *"One small step for man, one giant leap of faith for mankind. That was the story of Corbin Carpenter... The accident isn't what made him so popular, however, it was his*

unbelievable recovery that caught the nations heart…With the "Say I Won't" attitude Corbin took on therapy with great courage…Corbin's miraculous story spread like wild fire and inspired the lives of many…If you never knew Corbin Carpenter, you missed out. Those who were lucky enough to know him admired him for his recovery, but Corbin was so much more than that. The accident was a chapter of his life; it didn't define him. He was loved for his constant smile and sense of humor. Whether he was picking the guitar and making up songs as he went, or sweeping the National Rodeo Queen off her feet, there was never a dull moment when he was around. Thinking back, I can't remember a time where I didn't see a smile on his face. Even during the difficult times at the hospital in Farmington, he managed to flash his dimples for visitors…This article is not intended to be the story of his tragic death, instead, I want to celebrate the life Corbin had. Some people live their whole lives and never witness a miracle. Corbin, however, was a walking, talking, comedic, guitar playing, horse riding, inspiring, miracle. Because of his faith and strength he allowed the entire rodeo world to witness God's power. As the captain of the Bloomer team, and a Louisiana National rodeo team member, he lived his life fully...I hope that instead of questioning the Lord, we can have faith in His plan, even when it is impossible to understand. If you weren't fortunate enough to know Corbin, I hope you can be inspired by his life and true cowboy attitude."

Kallan Mudd
Kallan's Korner, Rodeo News,
October 15, 2010

Theresa Freeman Carpenter

Cowboy in the Sky

He wasn't here for very long,
And not nearly long enough.
But he was strong in heart and will,
He was truly cowboy tough.
So many hearts his life has touched,
So many things he overcame.
And after knowing him, I must say,
My life is not the same,
I know it hurts and I know it's hard,
But keep your head held high.
Because he was just our borrowed angel,
Now he's our cowboy in the sky.

Kallan Mudd
Kallan's Korner, Rodeo News,
October 15, 2010

Two Louisiana high school rodeo clubs paid tribute to Corbin in the spring of 2011. The first was my boy's home club, The Northeast Louisiana High School Rodeo Club. It was the first rodeo back after the holiday break. President Johnny Poole asked Colt to lead Pud around the arena with Corbin's boots placed backwards in the stirrups depicting tribute paid to a fallen Calvary soldier. As Colt was leading Pud, our good friend and cowboy minister, Scott Fletcher, talked about what a fine Christian Corbin was, the inspiration he was to others, plus made many other nice comments. I dare say there was a dry eye in the crowd, and many stood in Corbin's honor. Just before the memorial presentation, the club's high school seniors were recognized. Generally, the senior club member rides his/her horse around the arena as their pre-recorded farewell speech is played. Club member, Cari Dugdale, presented me with three red roses as her speech was being presented. In it, she paid tribute to Corbin and what an inspiration he has been to her. Thank you, Cari.

In March, 2011, we traveled to Gonzales, Louisiana, to the Southeastern Club Rodeo. I had been asked several weeks earlier if I would mind if they used the slogan "Ridin' for heaven's cowboy" on their t-shirts in honor of Corbin. Of course, I was elated that they wanted to do so. Once we arrived, I realized the entire rodeo was dedicated to him. The same slogan was used on their programs, and the club was wearing new royal blue shirts, Corbin's favorite color. What an honor it was for them to remember our sweet son in such a special way.

I have been told by many high school and junior high contestants, that they are riding this year for Corbin or in his memory. This is not only Louisiana kids, but the returning Bloomer Rodeo team will be wearing a blue ribbon in his memory as well. Another one that stands out in my mind is from a competitor in Alabama, Taylor Frazier. Taylor emailed me recently telling me that he lost his little roping mare recently and during each competiton, how he sees both his little mare and Corbin ringside as he rides. Taylor says he is rodeoing for both his horse and for Corbin this year.

❧

When remembering back on the many, wonderful memories we have made through the years traveling down the rodeo road, I recall a trip to the Sulphur, Louisiana arena one fall. The highway from near Forest Hill to Kinder, near I-10, has been under construction even prior to the time Corbin first began rodeoing. I remember him saying, "Do you think they will get this road finished before I graduate?"

To this day, they have not. Even now, as we travel this stretch, those words still ring in our ears.

Zach Wright, a bull rider who not only spent many days and nights at our house, has traveled to numerous rodeos with us. This particular day, we were traveling down that same stretch of highway to Suphur and the three boys, Colt, Corbin and Zack, were in the backseat, beginning to get somewhat rowdy as boys do. I called them down several times. Finally, I said in a stern voice, "OK, the next time we go to a high school rodeo, y'all are not comin' with us!" One can't imagine the startled looks that came from the back seat as they started to laugh!

Corbin finally said in a sarcastic tone, "Right. Without us, why would you even be going to a high school rodeo?"

Good point. We all laughed.

Zack is now wearing with pride, new chaps that he designed, and had custom made. The mahogany colored chaps with off white fringe bears "RIP Corbin" down the left leg with a cross embroidered behind Corbin's name. Zack says he prays before each ride, and thinks, "It ain't nothin' but a thing," one of Corbin's favorite sayings. Just before Zack nods his head for the gate to open he says, "Let's do it, Corbin."

Having not seen the chaps yet, I called his mom prior to writing this to get the details of them. She told me a story of which I was unaware, and wish to share in this writing. Penny, Zack's mom, said at the time Corbin was killed, Zack was entered in a Tri-State rodeo that Saturday night in Hineston, Louisiana. Because of the accident, Zack told his parents he wouldn't be riding that weekend. After the service at the cemetery on Saturday, Penny said it was total silence as they rode home. That is, until Zack said matter-of-factly and with authority, "I'm ridin' tonight."

His parents tried to persuade him otherwise because of his emotional state, but he was determined. That night, at the beginning of the Tri-State rodeo, they had a tribute to Corbin. When it came Zack's turn, according to his mom, he made one of the prettiest rides ever aboard a bull belonging to former professional bull rider, Bubba Dunn. He scored in the mid eighties, and won the bull riding. As Zack and his family rode home after the rodeo, his parents congratulated him on an awesome ride.

Zack said, "Corbin was riding with me tonight."

His mom told him she knew Corbin was there because they could feel his presence all around.

Zack said, "No. I mean he was really with me. I felt him holding onto the neck of my vest keeping me straight. I heard him whisper over and over 'Don't quit, don't quit.'"

Zack says Corbin rides each bull with him now, and he has the chaps to prove it.

While at the rodeo in Gonzales, spring 2011, Zach asked Dewitt to help him get on his bull. It would be the first time Dewitt had gone behind the rough stock chutes since he was there with Corbin. It proved to be hard for my husband, but I know Zach appreciated his help, and it meant a lot to him. Likewise, it meant a lot to Dewitt that he was asked. Thank you "Zack-a-rack."

Zack came off of his bull a little early that night, and got 'in a bind' doing so. When I later talked to him, I mentioned his guardian angel riding with him. He assured me Corbin was there.

∽

People of all ages, both young and old, seemed to flock to Corbin's electric personality. He had a smile that wouldn't stop, and one that would make his blue eyes dance. Corbin never intentionally hurt anyone's feelings, but rather lifted their spirits. He never set anyone apart in a manner that would make them feel beneath him or lesser of a person. I was reminded of this in a March 16, 2011 conversation

I had with long time friend and rodeo stock contractor, Jimmy Bergeron.

Mr. Jimmy said, "You know how young people are supposed to look up to older people? Well I'll tell you, I looked up to Corbin. He was an inspiration to everybody of any age."

Mr. Jimmy recalled, "The last time I really talked to him was the last night at the state rodeo finals (May 2011). He always called me Uncle Jimmy. After we talked for a while, he said, 'Uncle Jimmy, come on and let's go talk to some ladies.'" I said, "If you wanted Uncle Jimmy to go, you should have asked me at 7:00. It's Uncle Jimmy's bedtime now."

They laughed.

Mr. Jimmy went on, "My brother, Kenny, said he was amazed when we came up to Jonesville for the Black River rodeo the summer after he got hurt. Dewitt told Corbin to go load up thirty square bales of hay for us. He was by himself and just smiled that little smile and went and loaded the hay.

Kenny didn't even know Corbin was able to do it yet. That's just the way he was, he smiled that smile all the time."

As I recall, that was the year Bergeron Rodeo Company recognized Corbin during the Saturday night performance of the Black River Rodeo giving him a beautiful, leather hand crafted plaque, which read:

Corbin Carpenter

An Honorable Man,
An Inspiration To Us All. Thanks,

Bergeron Rodeo Company Family

As of this writing, we understand there will be a tribute made to Corbin during the Black River Roundup Rodeo to be held May 2011.

෧ර

I am told that a "Corbin Carpenter Day" is planned for the IFYR in Shawnee, OK for

2011. A scholarship will be given on that day set aside to honor Corbin's memory. Kim Bloomer told me that the returning members of the Bloomer Team will be wearing embroidered blue ribbons bearing Corbin's name on their team shirts. During that week, the Corbin Carpenter Memorial Foundation advisory board is planning to host a dummy roping in an effort to not only recognize Corbin but to raise money for whatever projects it undertakes.

It is also my understanding that a scholarship will be given by WESA to a deserving NHSRA senior during the NHSFR in Gillette, Wyoming, in July 2011. I am hopeful this will be an annual scholarship to help insure Corbin's legacy lives on.

∽

Perhaps one of the greatest tributes to our son, was that within the first six months following his tragic death, there have been two baby boys born who are named after him. In early November 2010, Leigh-Ann, one of Corbin's nurses from Farmington who became a good friend, emailed me. Following is an excerpt from her email:

> "...I have some news to share with you of Corbin and yet another life he touched. One of my friends is due to have a baby on February 2nd. She is going to name her son Corbin!!!! She wants him to turn out to be an amazing kido just like your precious son ...What a testimony to the impact Corbin had while he was here!!!"

Sure enough, on February 7, 2011, Josh and Liz Coffman of Farmington, New Mexico, named their first child, Corbin Kade Coffman. In a card written to me by his mom, she reiterated what Leigh-Ann had written to me a few months earlier.

Then, on March 18, 2011, Corey Colvin, a bull rider friend of Corbin's, and his wife named their precious son, Corbin Lane Colvin. Not only is this little cowboy's name Corbin, but he has the same initials, CLC.

My personal thanks to these two families for insuring our son's legacy lives on. What a tribute.

During the wake and funeral, we had note cards set up on a table at the entrance of the church hoping people would write their favorite memory or story about Corbin. We were amazed at some of the things people wrote. Without writing the names of those who wrote them, a few of the cards written are as follows:

> "He was always a good person to me, always prayed with us all. Always made me happy to see him."

> "Corbin was a huge inspiration on everyone, even if they didn't know him. If you were upset about a bad (rodeo) run he'd pick you up and tell you there is another rodeo. We were at Nationals and had gone to Hooters to eat and at the end of the meal he picked up my bill and told me he was buying because it was his turn and he was proud of me. I was so grateful and he did it out of true

generosity. He touched my heart in many ways"

"Dear Corbin, We've had a blast together. You're the only person who could tell me I was doing bad things, smile, then drive us to dinner. You are a great person. I'll always remember you and how we wore out and knew every word to Medagascar II "Maurice." Say a prayer and help me to be better. I love you."

"I will always remember Corbin's positive attitude and his smiling face. I can't remember a single time seeing Corbin angry or getting mad."

"What I remember most about Corbin was every time you saw him he was always smiling or cutting up or making jokes with you. He was a great person to be around, he would always keep you laughing. There was never a dull moment when you were with Corbin. He was one of my best pals and my favorite roping partner I have ever had. We may not have won state or nationals but I can promise you we had a great time doing what we loved! Corbin had more self drive than anyone I have ever met and if he set his mind to it he could do anything. I loved him like a brother and I love you, the family."

"Well man, you lived a good nineteen years. You served God as good as He could ask. You lead more people to the Lord and gave them hope with the things you did. I know deep in my heart that it was your time and that you was ready, your purpose was done. I'm gonna miss playing the guitar and laughing and having fun. Corbin you're my hero. I love you, buddy. You're a true friend and as cowboy as they come."

"I have dealt with many kids in my many years of teaching school and rodeoing and Corbin was definitely one that stood out among the rest. He always had that same smile on his face, and was so respectful and sweet. You should be so proud as parents that we were all blessed to have the opportunity to know such a wonderful kid. There are not many like Corbin this day and time. He will be greatly missed and in my opinion, will be a legend for many other kids to try to follow his example."

"I remember how Corbin cheered so loud and was so proud of his little brother, he was so proud of him every time he competed in the Wrangler Division. Corbin never gave up. He kept his pride so well and never wanted anyone to see his weakness."

"Corbin was always the one who could always make you smile. He always had high spirits and would tell you to pray about whatever your problems were."

"He would always have that big smile on his face. He always made us laugh. We loved to cut up and have fun with him. Corbin is our role model! We all love him!"

"I can honestly say that I never walked past Corbin without him stopping to shake my hand and wish me luck. He was the most respectful man, and I can't remember him not trying to motivate everyone around him! He is an inspiration to us all! My thoughts and prayers go out to his family and friends. Kneeling behind the chutes beside him to pray together before we rode was one of the greatest privileges of my life, and I'm gonna miss that probably more than anything."

"You're my superman and my inspiration. I'll never forget driving to McDonald's really late at nationals after cowboy prom. You and Colt were telling us jokes. When I got back, and told my mom who I was with, she ignored the fact I missed curfew because it was you...."

"Corbin made us all better people by knowing him. The first time I met him, I knew he would make a special impact on my life! Oh how he did!"

"He always had a smile on his face and when he would be with you he was able to put a smile on yours. Words cannot describe how good of a man he was because there aren't enough. I remember sittin' around playing guitars. We would just make up songs about anything that would come to mind. Every song was a Nashville hit and every word was gold!"

"Corbin has taught me a lot. God does things for a reason. He always told me to keep on trucking and never give up. Cowboy up."

"I loved your little mare, Puddin. My hat's off to you, buddy, for training such a good calf horse. I always respected you, man, for the great Christian cowboy you were."

"He was an angel loaned to us to guide and teach us. His smile will never be forgotten, always in my heart, Corbin. Ride cowboy, ride."

"At Nationals 2009, Corbin and Jake were playing guitar and while Jake played, Corbin asked the National Rodeo Queen to dance with him. It was the sweetest thing ever!"

"I could fill this stack of cards with all of the fantastic memories I had with Corbin. He was a pizza eatin', guitar playin', story tellin', make everyone in the room laugh till they cried fool! ....I love you, Corbin."

"...When we were very young and the Carpenter family and our family were going somewhere. We were getting very loud and his mom said that all bad little children would be dropped off at the "kid jail" while the adults went on to have a good time. Corbin assured us there was such a place because he had been there. To this day, I don't know if he was just playing along with his mom, or he had really been in trouble."

"My first memory of Corbin was at the Lazy T. I was ribbon roping with him.

I was so nervous and my heart was beatin' so fast. Corbin just told me to 'breathe.' Then he told me all he had to do was catch the calf and I had the hard part. Just get the ribbon and run and don't fall down. Then he smiled…"

∽

In a recent email I received from Taci Shaffer, the former NHSR rodeo queen from Utah, she had this to say: "There is so much I could say about Corbin. First of all, he was the most genuine person I have ever known. Being around Corbin just brought so much joy to my heart. It is so true what they say, 'the good die young,' because he was full of goodness. Just the light in his life that he would share with anyone he was around, was more than words could speak for…."

∽

Corbin always treated everyone in such a way that made them feel good about themselves. I can remember numerous times when a fellow bull rider or roper would make a careless mistake and talk to Corbin about it. He would try to pick them up by telling them how well they handled the situation and how he would have probably done something totally different that would have had worse results, knowing in my heart had the tables been turned, he wouldn't have handled the situation that way at all. But that was Corbin, always trying to make people feel good about themselves. Perhaps that is partly the reason he was so loved. I remember during the wake, the night prior to Corbin's funeral, a good friend and fellow bull rider, Cody "Too Tall" Morgan told me of just such an example. In writing this book, and not wanting to rely on my own memory, I emailed Cody, asking him to again give me the details of the story to insure it's correctness for this book. I asked his permission to include his story. Many, many stories have been told to us in the days following Corbin's death that mirror his sense of encouragement to others. Cody replied:

> "...yes mam, I remember it like it was yesterday. My junior year I had rode pretty much everything I got on and was loaded with confidence. That's

when I met Corbin. He came up to me at Ruston and told me he liked my attitude and the way I rode. He made my head swell like a balloon! That was like the fourth or fifth rodeo of the year. He was a freshman and I really didn't know who he was, just some skinny kid from Jonesville. But it made me feel good and I told myself 'I like that kid' and made a mental note to watch him ride from then on. Time went on and the more I watched him, the more I learned from him. At the time, I really didn't know what was so special about him or what stood out in my mind the most about him, but I knew he was a hand and a cowboy down to the ground. We became pretty close and I knew anytime I needed advice, I could ask Corbin and whatever it was, he told me the honest truth whether I wanted to hear it or not. Whether I rode good or not, Corbin always told me the positive about whatever I did. About halfway through my senior year, I was in a horrible slump I had hardly made points to get on the board. Every bull I got on, it seemed was throwing me off. I couldn't even seem to stay on the weakest bull in the herd. I remember we were in Jena and I had drawn a bull I had ridden two or three times and had won both times on him. He was just a good bull, spun both ways, had lots of timing, just one you wanna have. I told Corbin before I got on that 'things have got to get better tonight. I'm wearin' my lucky shirt and I've ridden this bull before so, it's on champ, just watch! 'I no more than knodded my head. That bull cracked it in the gate and put me on my head, stepped down on my arm and tore my shirt to no end. I crawled to the fence with a brand new hat ruined and my lucky shirt was ruined, too. I dragged myself out of the pen and sat down behind the chutes. I was pretty disgusted and down. The rodeo ended and I was packing my stuff. Corbin walks up and I said, 'Man, I don't know what's wrong with me. I can't seem to stay on anything. It tore my lucky shirt and on a bull I've rode before.'

He looked at me and said, "Cody, the shirt's not lucky. You made the shirt seem that way by the way you wore it and shined. You made your own luck 'cause you had faith, no matter what happened, you knew in the end God had you. Just keep the faith and keep working at it."

Right then and there it hit me. That's what made Corbin so tough. He had more faith than any man or woman I had ever met. And he proved it to the world before he left this earth. As long as I live I'll never forget him."

Cody Morgan

Chapter 16

With the loss of our son-in-law in April and then Corbin five months and two days later, a year like we experienced in 2010 has proven to be one we obviously never wish to repeat. With each passing day, my prayers have been that God would be merciful to us, and not take other members of my family. However, I realize from this two things. First of all, I am being selfish. As Christians, both Wyatt and Corbin are in a far better place than we can ever imagine. They now dwell with our Lord and Savior Jesus Christ. They have seen His face, and touched His nail scarred hands. As Christians, we long to live in this land where there will be no more tears and no more sorrow; a place where we too, can touch the face of God.

Looking back, we feel Corbin knew something big was about to happen from the conversations he had had with some of his friends and things he said. I'm not sure what you call this, sort of a premonition, I suppose, but both Corbin and I could many times feel when something was about to happen. We discussed it many times, and both agreed that we hated that unsettled feeling. In several of our conversations regarding this, I told him perhaps it is God preparing us for what is ahead.

Before we lost Wyatt, I had a horrible feeling for months prior that something was going to happen to someone close to me, even to the point that I would sometimes have an eerie feeling as I drove past our local funeral home. When Wyatt died, I thought that was what God had been preparing me for. However, I realized that was only part of it, as following Wyatt's death, periodically the feeling would continue to resurface.

Corbin never said anything to me about having this unsettled feeling before he died. However, we later found out he had said some things to his sister and a couple of his closest friends that now makes me believe he was experiencing this feeling. He and Courtney had a long conversation one night only a few weeks before he was killed. Corbin was crying, saying he missed Wyatt very much, and wanted to see him again. Courtney told him that we would all see him again someday. Corbin told her that she didn't understand, he longed to see him now. On another occasion, he and Slade Deason were together along this same timeframe. Corbin randomly told Slade that when he died he wanted Slade to lead Pud to his gravesite. He also told Colter White that if anything ever happened to him, not to cry; there would be no reason for him to.

Colt's little mare, Sugar, cut her leg badly just before the 2010-11 high school and junior high rodeo season started. Colt was upset because it was evident that he would be unable to ride his horse for several months. Although Corbin used Pud almost daily, he told Colt that he could ride her at each of the rodeos, and anytime he needed her. With that, Colt has rodeoed on Pud the entire 2010-11 season and although Sugar is ready to go again, I don't foresee him changing horses anytime soon. It was as though Corbin gave Colt permission to ride her going forth. Knowing how Corbin felt about Pud, I'm not sure that Colt would be riding her now had his big brother not told him it was okay.

A short while after Corbin's funeral, I found a scratch piece of paper on his chest-of-drawers, that simply said, "Matthew 24:36." I looked up the verse in the Bible and it reads:

> *"But of that day and hour knoweth no man, no not the angels of heaven, but my Father only."*

I believe God was preparing Corbin to leave this world and enter into eternity.

⁂

Anyone who knew Corbin would agree with me that he would not want any of us to mull in our grief for him. However, our hearts continue to break because we miss him terribly. Perhaps Colt described it best when he said, "If you took my heart, and divided it into pieces for each person I love, two pieces would be missing."

Like Wyatt, Corbin was a Christian, and because of the life he led, we know and accept that it was God's will for him to be called home. We know they are in a far better place than we can ever imagine. I heard a song recently that reiterates that fact. This beautiful song was written by an artist who lost his daughter in an auto accident some years ago. So I understand the story, his family was so distraught over their loss that this gentleman wrote this song in an effort to comfort them. It certainly did me when I heard the words. The title says it all; *"One Less Day on Earth Means One More Day in Heaven."*

God promises us, as Christians, we will again see our precious son someday, and because God said it, I believe that with all of my heart. Where Corbin is now, his neck no longer hurts, and his right side is stronger than ever. He is once again doing what he loves, riding the rankest bulls ever!

Secondly, we have been told by numerous people since Corbin's injury in 2008, and especially since the loss of our two boys, that our family has met more than it's fair share of tragedy. The fact is, the human side of us may think this to be so. I have never asked God "why" these things have happened to our family. I already know the answer...."why not?" Being a Christian does not exempt us from this or any further tragedies, it simply means that we have God to lean on, to give us the strength that gets us through each day. I recall Corbin saying many times following his injury that he didn't know how people got through such experiences without the Lord. I agree with him now more than ever.

> Therefore, since we have been justified through faith, we have peace with God through our Lord Jesus Christ, through whom we have gained access by faith into this grace in which we now stand. And we rejoice in the hope of the glory of God. Not sufferings, because we know that suffering produce perseverance; perseverance, character; and character, hope And hope does not disappoint us, because God has poured out His love into our hearts by the Holy Spirit, whom He has given us. Romans 5: 1-5 (NIV)

Many people, both young and old, have been saved since Corbin's injury. The testimony he continues to have, even today after his death, has touched many lives. I believe when our purpose for being on earth has been fulfilled, God calls us home. In 2 Timothy 4:5-7, Paul speaks of this.

> *"Keep your head in all situations, endure hardship, do the work of an evangelist, discharge all the duties of your ministry. For I am already being poured out like a drink offering, and the time has come for my departure. I have fought a good fight, I have finished my course, I have kept the faith. Now there is in store for me the crown of righteousness, which the Lord, the righteous Judge, will award to me on that day, and not only to me, but also to all who have longed for his appearing. 2 Timothy 4:5-7 (NIV)*

༄

Our daughter, Courtney, told me recently that since Corbin's bull riding accident, she had always wandered what awesome things God had in store for her brother, but didn't realize she was watching it everyday. As sad as we are, we trust God, and we know He sees the big picture. We cannot. It is because of this that we are able to draw strength from Him, and know regardless of what the future holds, we know **who** holds the future. I believe all things happen for a reason, and am reminded of the scripture in Romans 8:28 that all things work together for the good of those who love God.

> *And we know that in all things God works for the good of those who love Him, who have been called according to his purpose.*
> Romans 8:28 (NIV)

❦

We now meet each day with more challenge than ever before, but our trust in Jesus Christ sees us through, and gives us the faith and strength needed. As each of us has experienced at one time or the other, life is hard. How we chose to handle the problems and tragedies that arise is up to us as individuals. In every instance,

God is waiting for us to ask for His help, His guidance, and His love.

Our close friend, Bill Brown, built a glass showcase for the purpose of displaying Corbin's rodeo gear. It stands about six feet tall, three feet wide and two feet or so deep. This case is in our den and is a constant reminder that Corbin is still with us. It contains, Corbin's chaps, vest, bull riding glove, bull rope, riggin' bag, his hat, guitar, lariat ropes, a Bloomer Rodeo team shirt, and many of the back numbers he has worn through the years. It displays his bull riding boots with spurs still attached and also the boots he wore daily with roping spurs made by our friend, John Bache, still hanging from the heel in tack. Close beside his boots, lay the custom bull riding spurs, also made by John, that Corbin was so proud of but never had a chance to ride in. It also holds two of his belts he regularly wore with Champion belt buckles he won attached. One of the belts was hand painted by his friend, Corey Granger. Displayed beside his vest is the tattered and worn "The Way For Cowboys" Bible that Corbin carried in his riggin' bag for many years.

Theresa Freeman Carpenter

The day Bill brought the case to our house, Corbin's friend, Colten Blanchard from the Sulphur, Louisiana area, was visiting. We asked Colten to tie and hang in the case Corbin's bull rope. It was then we realized that Colten pulled Corbin's rope just before he bucked out on M33 at the 2008 NHSFR, the ride that proved to be Corbin's last competition ride. We found it ironic that Colten was the last person who pulled Corbin's rope, and now he would be the one to tie it and hang it in the showcase. It is through these many wonderful memories that God allows to surface, through special people and special things like Bill building the showcase, John making the spurs, and Colten being there to tie and hang Corbin's rope, that keep us close to our son. Not only do we continue to keep Corbin in our hearts, but we feel Jesus' loving arms wrapped tightly around us everyday. God is in control of everything, this is no exception.

It is true for anyone who knew Corbin, that once you met him, your life was never the same. We were very blessed to have had him with us for nineteen years and to be able to call him our son. Our true peace is knowing Corbin is spending eternity in heaven.

> *"Peace I leave with you; my peace I give you. I do not give to you as the world gives. Do not let your hearts be troubled and do not be afraid."*
> John 14:27 (NIV)

As I am writing these final words of this chapter, it has been seven months since we lost our precious son. Winter has turned to spring, the days lengthen, and are becoming warmer. It is spring calving time at the Bar CC. As we ride through the pastures checking cattle, we realize this is a job Corbin would have been doing, either with us or alone. As we gaze across the green pastures, we see the fences Corbin has mended, the old cow he and Colt doctored last summer that now has a calf by her side, and we remember the many hours we all shared together on the ranch, both working and playing. The horses we ride while checking cattle can be trusted because Corbin's gentle hands are the ones that broke and trained them. As I am riding, with each ray from the sun that shines down upon me, I feel as though it is Corbin's sweet smile warming my heart, and I can feel him riding along beside me. I hear his laughter dancing from each gentle breeze that blows. We miss our precious Corbin more than ever but we know he is safe in the arms of God. Until we see him again in heaven, we'll be praising God for the countless memories, the endless love Corbin left with us, and each time we saddle up, we know we will be forever *'ridin' with heaven's cowboy....'*

Scars heal, times passes, memories fade...but legends last forever.
We're ridin' for ya, buddy.

Jake Hebert

Live like you're dancing with
Gorillas!!!

Heaven's Cowboy

The photograph on the previous page was taken during an interview with professional rodeo commentator, Pam Minick, during the Bloomer Trailer Rodeo Team meeting, April 2010.

(Photo courtesy of Just The Way You Are)

The Carpenters can be reached by email at carpenterbarcc@aol.com

38029615R00142

Made in the USA
Charleston, SC
29 January 2015